Cooking with Exotic Fruit

Cooking with Exotic Fruit

Selma and W.J.A. Payne

Illustrations by Alistair Payne

B.T. Batsford Ltd. London

First published 1979
© Selma and W.J.A. Payne
ISBN 0 7134 1192 9

Typeset by Tek-Art Ltd, London SE20
Printed by William Clowes Ltd, Beccles, Suffolk
for the Publishers B T Batsford Ltd,
4 Fitzhardinge Street, London W1H OAH

Contents

Notes on using the recipes

As very few fruits produced in the tropics are graded, individual fruits often vary considerably in size. This makes it difficult to propose the use of a specific number of fruits in specific recipes. This difficulty has been to some extent overcome by the use of volume measurements for fruit juice and/or pulp, once the fruits have been initially processed.

Both metric and imperial weights, volumes and temperatures are given in the recipes. As volume measurements can be misleading unless they are related to measured volumes (because cups, tablespoons and teaspoons vary in size from household to household), the measured volume equivalents of the receptacles used in these recipes is shown below.

ordinary glass (tumbler)	300 ml
whisky glass	175 ml
teacup	150 ml
dessertspoon	10 ml
teaspoon	4 ml

To test whether the setting point of jam or jelly has been reached, put a small spoonful of the cooking mixture on a plate and let it cool. If when cool the mixture wrinkles up when the plate is tipped or when the jam is pushed with a fingertip, it is ready. If a cooking thermometer is used, the jam or jelly will set when the thermometer reads 105°C (221°F).

Introduction

On first arriving in the tropical island that was to become our home for many years we visited the local fruit market, only to be bewildered by vast arrays of fruits that we had never seen or even heard of before. Although we were informed that they were all edible, we played safe by buying the bananas, pineapples and citrus fruits that we were familiar with. But even these often looked and usually tasted quite differently from those we had bought from the greengrocer down the road, at home in England. Slowly we learned the names of the fruits so new to us and discovered how they could be used. It was particularly delightful to find that fresh fruit was available all the year round and to discover how delicious some of these, unknown in this country, could taste. It was even more rewarding to find that many of these were growing in the garden, unrecognized during those first few months.

Twenty-five years later, now living in England but frequent visitors to the tropics, we are always meeting people overseas who confess that they have the same problem as we did initially. They see an infinite variety of fruits in the local market which they can neither identify nor use. It was from our own early predicament and from the queries of a new generation of expatriates that the idea of this book of recipes for tropical fruits was conceived. Since there are an extraordinary number of tropical fruits, many completely unknown outside a particular region, we reluctantly decided that we would have to restrict ourselves to writing about a limited number of them. The fruits included here are therefore those that are the most widely used in the tropics, and the recipes those with which we are most familiar.

Although the book is designed primarily as a recipe book, we believe that, unlike most recipe books, it should also provide other useful and relevant information. The common English names for the fruits are used in all the recipes, but their botanical name, along with their names in all the principal European languages used in the tropics, and some indigenous ones are also provided. There are brief descriptions of the fruits and the plants that produce them, together with drawings prepared by our son, Alistair, who was born and grew up in the tropics, that should assist the reader in identification. Some interesting information is also provided on the origin and history of these fruits and on the localities in which they now grow. Finally, some notes are provided on cultivation, especially for those enthusiasts who may become interested in growing tropical fruits in their own garden, as we ourselves did.

Selma and W.J.A. Payne

1 *Avocado* *Persea americana*

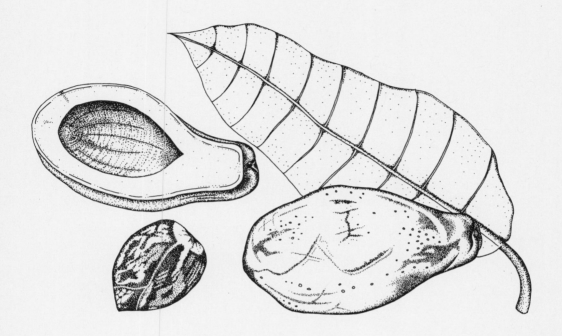

Other names that may be used

Other botanical names: *Laurus indicus, Persea gratissima, Persea praecox*
Dutch: advocaat
Other English: alligator pear, avocado-pear, soldier's butter
French: avocat, avocatier, poire d'avocat
Indian subcontinent languages: anakoya-pallam (Tamil); et-pera (Singalese)
Portuguese: abacate (Brazil)
Southeast Asian languages: advokat (Indonesian); aguacate (Tagalog); a-wo-kha-do
    (Thai); buah mēntenga, palta (Malaysian)
Spanish: aguacate, aguacate pera, aguacatillo (Venezuela); ahucate, ahuacath
    (Mexico); paltas, palta (Peru); palto (Chile, Peru)
West African languages: am-pier (Temne); bolbia, bombia (Mende); pia (Creole)

Where it grows
Although avocado will grow any where in the tropics and the warmer subtropics

9

where there is a well-distributed rainfall or where irrigation is available, within the tropics it thrives best in upland areas or in lowland areas with a monsoon climate. Different varieties are adapted to different climates. The West Indian variety and some of its hybrids, for example, are adapted to lowland tropics where the annual rainfall may be as high as 2,500 mm (98 in). The Guatemalan varieties are adapted to the upland tropics and the Mexican ones to upland sup-tropical areas; both types are adapted to climates where the rainfall can be as low as 750 to 1,000 mm (30 to 40 in) per annum.

Description

It is a medium-sized evergreen tree, 2 to 6 m (6 to 20 ft) in height, with a brown, roughish bark and a canopy that varies from low, dense and symmetrical to upright and straggly. The branches are brittle and are easily broken by strong winds.

Avocado leaves are 8 to 25 cm (3 to 10 in) long; they vary in shape and are bunched together at the end of the twigs. They are often hairy and reddish when young, but as they mature become smooth, leathery and dark green on the upper surface while a dull, whitish-green underneath. The leaves of the Mexican variety possess a very distinctive smell like anise.

The flowers are small, pleasant smelling and yellowish-green, and are borne on long branches.

An avocado fruit consists of a large single seed, loosely enclosed in a central cavity and surrounded by a buttery pulp. The fruits hang on drooping stalks, usually several at the end of one twig, and they vary greatly in size, shape, colour, skin thickness and texture, and flavour.

Their weight may range from 115g to 2½ kg (¼ to 5 lb), and in size they can be 7 to 20 cm (3 to 8 in) long and 7 to 10 cm (3 to 4 in) in diameter. They may be almost round, oval or pear-shaped. When the fruit is mature, its skin varies from a brilliant or yellowish-green to a deep green speckled with white, or it may be black, purple or reddish. The outer skin of the fruit may be smooth, rough and papery, leathery or woody. The edible pulp varies in colour from almost white, through a buttery-yellow to a yellowish-green.

Avocadoes do not ripen until they are about to fall, so they should be picked just before they ripen. Ripening occurs three to eight days after picking. The most suitable temperature for ripening is 16° to 24°C (60° to 75°F), and so once picked they should be kept in a cool place until they are ready to eat.

Origin and history

Avocadoes probably originated in the tropical region of the American continent that is now Ecuador and Colombia. They were apparently introduced into Peru by the Incas some time during the latter half of the fifteenth century and into southern Mexico in the thirteenth to fifteenth centuries by the Aztecs. Columbus and the other early Spanish explorers never noted this fruit in the West Indies, but the Conquistadores wrote of its availability on the continent from Peru to Mexico and as far east as Venezuela.

The Spanish introduced the avocado into the West Indian islands, the Mediterranean countries and probably into the Philippines in the seventeenth century, but it never became a popular fruit in southern Europe. The cultivation of avocadoes spread slowly throughout the West Indies. It was introduced into Jamaica in 1650, where the Spanish name was anglicized to 'avocado' by 1696. At the end of the eighteenth century it was known in Mauritius and Hawaii, but its cultivation was very slow in spreading to the African and Asiatic mainlands, primarily because the avocado seed remains viable for only a few weeks after the fruit has ripened. In the nineteen-twenties, commercial planting of avocadoes began in South Africa, Argentina and Israel. The avocado was first introduced into North America via Florida in 1833 and in 1871 to California. Commerical planting, however, began in North America only at the beginning of the present century.

Notes on cultivation

Avocadoes grow best in deep, fertile, well-drained soils, particularly slightly acid, sandy and alluvial loams. The tree is extremely sensitive to poor drainage and is intolerant of salty soils. It may be grown from seed, which should be sown as soon as possible after the fruit is ripe, but commercial farmers propagate it vegetatively by budding or grafting. Planting distances range from 6 by 8 m (20 by 26 ft) to 10 by 20 m (33 by 39 ft), according to whether the variety is upright or spreading. Avocadoes are fertilized in the same way as citrus trees and are rarely pruned. In orchards, windbreaks are desirable as the branches are very brittle, and ladders should not be used when picking the fruit. The trees can be intercropped, those propagated from seed bearing their first fruit at about seven years of age, and budded or grafted trees after about three to four years. Mature trees will produce 100 to 500 fruits each year and good commerical orchards yield 1,100 to 2,200 kg/ha (6,000 to 12,000 lb/acre) of fruit. The most serious disease of avocadoes is root rot.

General uses and recipes

Avocado is a fine salad fruit, though some people consider it an acquired taste. It has a high nutritive value, with an oil content of 3 to 30 per cent, and contains medium to large amounts of carotene. The fruit is usually cut in half and the pulp then scooped out with a spoon. It may be eaten plain or flavoured with salt, pepper, vinegar, Worcestershire sauce, sherry or whatever takes the fancy. The pulp can be mashed and mixed with condiments to make a sandwich spread or filling and the fruit can also be used in a variety of recipes.

AVOCADO SALAD

1 beetroot
1 sprig finely-chopped mint or
   1 stick celery
salt and pepper

2 medium avocadoes
French dressing or lemon juice
1 lettuce

Cook the beetroot, peel and dice it while hot. Allow to cool then mix the mint or celery with the diced beetroot and season it with salt and pepper. Cut the avocadoes crossways into 4 circular sections. Remove the stone and any skin that may come loose with it. Pour the dressing or lemon juice over the avocado sections. Arrange lettuce leaves on a plate and set the circular sections of the avocado on them. Place the beetroot mixture in the centre of the avocado sections and chill.

AVOCADO FRUIT SALAD

1 grapefruit
1 orange
1 mango

1 medium avocado
salad dressing or mayonnaise

Peel the grapefruit and the orange, skin the mango and cut all into cubes. Cut the avocado in half lengthways; remove the stone and any skin that may come loose from the stone. Peel and cut into 2 cm (¾ in) cubes. Mix them with the fruit. Chill the mixture. Serve the salad with salad dressing or mayonnaise, according to taste.

AVOCADO COCKTAIL (1)

1 medium avocado
1 grapefruit or ripe papaya
cream or top of the milk

tomato sauce or Worcestershire sauce
lemon juice

Cut the avocado in half lengthways; remove the stone and any skin that may come loose from it. Peel the halves and cut the flesh into 2 cm (¾ in) cubes. Peel the grapefruit or the papaya, cut the flesh into cubes and mix them with the avocado. Pour the cream or milk over the mixture. Add the sauce and lemon juice according to taste. Chill.

AVOCADO COCKTAIL (2)

1 medium avocado
½ medium pineapple

1 dessertspoon of fresh coconut
French dressing

Cut the avocado in half lengthways; remove its stone and any skin that may come loose from it. Peel the halves and cut the flesh into 2 cm (¾ in) cubes. Cut the skin from the pineapple, remove the eyes, take out the core and chop the flesh. Mix the pineapple with the avocado. Grate the coconut and sprinkle over the mixed fruit. Chill. Serve with French dressing to taste.

AVOCADO COCKTAIL (3)

4 medium avocadoes
salt
½ teaspoon chopped onion

2 teaspoons vinegar or lemon juice
½ cup tomato sauce (either home made or purchased ketchup)

Cut the avocadoes in half lengthways; remove the stones and any skin that may come loose from them. Peel the halves and cut the flesh into 2 cm (¾ in) cubes. Add salt to taste and chill in a covered dish. Combine the onion, vinegar and tomato sauce and chill. Pour this mixture over the fruit just before serving.

CURRIED AVOCADO

2 medium avocadoes
30 gm (1 oz) fat
1 medium onion

1 heaped tablespoon flour
1 tablespoon curry powder
285 ml (½ pint) milk

Cut in half and remove the stone and any skin that may have come loose from it. Peel the halves and cut the flesh into cubes. Place on one side in a covered dish. Melt the fat in a saucepan. Chop the onion and add the chopped onion to the fat. Fry until the onion is slightly brown. Add the flour, the curry powder and the milk slowly and stir until the sauce thickens. Add the chopped avocado to the sauce. (Do not boil the avocado or it will taste bitter.) Serve hot on toast or rice.

AVOCADO WITH CREAMED FISH

2 medium avocadoes
115 g (4 oz) tin of fish (tuna, salmon, crabmeat or shrimp)
salt and pepper

White sauce:
30 g (1 oz) fat
1 heaped tablespoon flour
425 ml (¾ pint) milk

Cut the avocadoes in half lengthways and remove the stones. To make the white sauce, melt the fat in a saucepan, add the flour and stir until it thickens. Stir in the milk slowly so that there are no lumps. Bring to the boil and simmer for a minute or two. Add the fish, salt and pepper to the white sauce. Fill the avocado halves with the mixture. Place them under a grill until they are brown or heat them in an oven for 5 to 15 minutes at 180°C (350°F), Gas Mark 4.

AVOCADO MOUSSE WITH SHRIMPS

1 packet lime jelly to make
   570 ml (1 pint)
285 ml (½ pint) water
3 medium avocadoes
3 tablespoons lemon juice

¼ cup mayonnaise
2 tablespoons grated onions
½ teaspoon salt and pepper
¾ cup whipped cream
shrimps

Cut the jelly into small pieces. Boil the water, pour it over the jelly, mix until dissolved and cool. Peel the avocadoes, remove the stones and pass the flesh through a sieve. Add the lemon juice, mayonnaise, onion, and salt and pepper to taste to the sieved avocado. Mix. Fold the whipped cream into the avocado mixture and add the cooled jelly. Mix until well blended and set in a mould. Chill. Turn the mousse out, when set, on to a serving dish. Marinate the shrimps in lemon juice for 30 mins. Serve them on top of the mousse.

AVOCADO SANDWICH SPREAD

½ cup mashed avocado
½ teaspoon grated onion
a dash of Worcestershire sauce

a squeeze of lemon
salt and pepper to taste

Mix all the ingredients into the avocado with a fork. Use the avocado mixture as a sandwich filling.

AVOCADO ICE-CREAM

2 medium avocadoes
¼ cup sugar
¼ teaspoon salt

¼ teaspoon celery salt (optional)
⅓ cup lemon, lime or kalamansi
   juice

Peel the avocadoes, remove the stones and pass the flesh through a sieve. Add the sugar to the sieved fruit with the salts and the fruit juice. Blend. Freeze in ice-trays for 2 to 4 hours, taking out the mixture when half-set and whipping it once during the freezing time.

BRAZILIAN AVOCADO COOLER

1 medium avocado (papaya or banana
   can be substituted)
sugar

1 to 2 cups cold milk
1 teaspoon lemon juice
twists of lemon or orange rind,
   or mint to garnish

Peel the avocado, remove the stone and dice the flesh. Place it in a blender or pass
it through a sieve. Sweeten the avocado with sugar to taste. Add the milk and
lemon juice gradually to the avocado mixture while blending or stirring. Serve
in tall chilled glasses garnished with the lemon or orange twists or sprigs of
fresh mint.

2 Banana

There are three major types of cultivated banana.

Musa paradisiaca var. *sapientum* should be considered a collective botanical name for a large number of cultivated varieties that may have developed from more than one wild ancestor. The fruit from these bananas is edible when raw. *Musa chinensis*: synonyms, *Musa cavendishii*, *Musa nana* is the Chinese or dwarf type of banana that is also edible when raw. *Musa paradisiaca* is the cooking banana or plantain.

Other names that may be used

Dutch: bakove (Surinam); banaan
French: banane, bananier
Indian subcontinent languages: kehel (Singalese); vala (Tamil)
Pacific languages: banana; viemama; plantain; vudi (Fijian)
Portuguese: banana
Southeast Asian languages: kluai (Thai); pisang (Malaysian and Indonesian);
    pisang tandok (plaintain in Malaysian)
Spanish: banano (Venezuela); guineo (Panama and Colombia); platano; minimo
    (Honduras)
West African languages: Banana: akodu, kodu (Ewe); ayabar daji (Hausa); kodu
    (Krobo); kwadu (Twi); ma-banana (Temne); ogede (Yoruba); ogede-ntiti,
    unere (Ibo); sele, selei (Mende) *Plantain:* abladzo (Ewe); ayaba (Hausa);
    e-planti, e-santi (Temne); kontomboli (Fula); mana, manei, maa (Mende);
    manaa, madaa (Krobo); oborode (Twi); ogede (Ibo); ogede-agbagba
    (Yoruba); plantin (Creole)

Where it grows

The bananas, which are edible raw, and the plantains will grow in suitable soils
in all lowland, humid, tropical regions and in drier areas where irrigation is available. Dwarf bananas will also grow in some humid subtropical areas and above
1,000 m (3,300 ft) in the humid tropics.

Description

Bananas are really gigantic herbs whose true stem is a large underground rhizome
and whose leaves grow out from ground level, their ends closely overlapping and
arranged in a spiral to form a type of trunk. After the fruit has ripened this
trunk is cut down. Suckers develop around the base of the first trunk and form a
series of new trunks that bear fruit in succession.

Heights vary with some plantains growing up to 4½ m (15 ft). The leaves
of the *sapientum* varieties and the plantains may be a deep-green or greenish-
yellow. The dwarf ones have shorter, broader leaves, often spotted reddish or
yellow when the plants are young. The leaves of all bananas tear easily and
become tattered and ragged in windy localities.

Once the flower head emerges from the trunk it normally droops. The
conical pointed tip contains the male flowers, while the female flowers that
develop into the fruits are spirally grouped behind the male ones. The flowers
are protected by purple bracts that drop off as the flower head develops.

The fruits are normally seedless, differing in size, shape and flavour, and
the outer skin may be greenish-yellow, yellow, reddish-yellow or red. The half-

17

spirals of fruit that develop from the female flowers are known as a 'hand', while individual fruits are called 'fingers'.

Origin and history

The banana was possibly one of the first plants to be cultivated by man. It appears to have originated in one of the mountainous regions of Southeast Asia: either in Assam, Burma, Thailand or Indo-China.

It was widely cultivated in India in early historical times, where according to legend the wise old men rested in the shade thrown by its leaves and ate the fruit. Hence the botanical name — *Musa sapientum* — fruit of the wise men. In Europe, it was known in both Greek and Roman times, having been introduced into western Asia by the Arabs. It was also widely distributed in the Pacific region before the advent of Europeans. In the sixteenth century it was cultivated in the Canary Islands and was first taken from these islands to the Americas by Friar Tomas de Berlanga, who introduced it into Santo Domingo in 1516. Within a short space of time bananas were grown throughout the Caribbean region and had been introduced into Mexico and other tropical mainland American countries.

Notes on cultivation

Bananas thrive best in well-drained, moist, fertile soils. As banana leaves are easily torn by wind and the plant is shallow-rooted, commerical plantations are not normally located in very windy areas nor in the major hurricane zones.

The plant is propagated vegetatively from suckers, and it is normal to utilize, for planting, suckers that produce a base shoot some 1 m (3¼ ft) high. Average planting distances are 4½ m² (15 ft²) for the large varieties and 3½ m² (12 ft²) for the dwarf varieties. Holes 46 cm² (18 in²) are first dug and filled with compost and top-soil in which the suckers are then planted. Bananas respond well to both organic and inorganic fertilizers. With good management and on fertile soil, bananas will fruit for the first time at 9 to 12 months of age. As the first stem matures, suckers appear around it. These should be pruned so that only four remain at any one time; one fruiting, one about to fruit, one half-grown and one just commencing growth. In humid areas this practice ensures a succession of fruiting stems at approximately three-month intervals. Where there is a marked dry season, there will be longer intervals between stems fruiting during the drier months, and the soil around the plant should be mulched before the dry season commences.

Under commercial conditions the life-span of a banana plantation is 5 to 20 years, but under garden conditions individual plants may continue to yield for 50 to 60 years. Flower heads produce 5 to 20 hands containing 2 to 20 fingers in each hand. Average bunches weigh 16 to 36 kg (35 to 80 lb) and comprise 120 to 200 individual bananas.

There are numerous varieties. Well-known large eating bananas include Gros Michel and Robusta, while Canary, Lacatan and Lady's Finger are popular medium-sized ones.

The most important diseases and pests of the banana are Sigatoka disease, Panama disease, bunchy-top virus, root rot, banana borers and nematodes.

General uses and recipes

Apart from producing fruit, bananas have other uses. A species known as *Musa textilis* is used for the production of the fibre, abaca or Manila hemp. In many regions of the tropics, banana leaves are used as a wrapping for other foods and as a substitute for a plate. The stems, chopped down after the fruit has been harvested, are succulent feed for ruminant livestock. The flower of some varieties makes an excellent side dish when cooked in coconut cream.

Unripe bananas have a high starch content. These and plantains may be either boiled or fried; they can be dried and ground into a flour, or fermented to make a beer.

As bananas ripen there is a decline in the starch content and an increase in sucrose and other sugars. Ripe bananas may be peeled and eaten raw, dried or used in other recipes.

BANANA COCKTAIL

1 ripe banana
½ tablespoon vinegar or lemon juice
1 teaspoon finely-chopped celery
½ teaspoon Worcestershire sauce
1 tablespoon tomato ketchup (home-made or purchased ketchup)
salt and pepper to taste

Peel and dice the banana. Add the remaining ingredients, mix, chill and serve in a glass or in a scooped-out green pepper.

BAKED BANANAS

6 large, ripe bananas
water
butter
salt and pepper to taste

Cover the bottom of a baking pan with water, wash the bananas and place them in the tin so that they are half-covered by the water. Bake at 180°C (350°F), Gas Mark 4 for 30 minutes or until the bananas are soft and their skins have burst. Serve them with butter, salt and pepper.

BANANA CHIPS

20 green cooking bananas (plantains)
1 cup white sugar

⅓ teaspoon salt
oil or fat for deep frying

Peel and slice the bananas thinly, lengthways. Mix the sugar and salt together on a plate. Dip each banana slice in the sugar-salt mixture and drop it into the boiling fat. Cook quickly; take chips out when crisp and drain on kitchen paper. Cool the chips and store them in air-tight containers.

BANANA BLOSSOM

Only the blossom of certain bananas can be used in this recipe. Information on suitable varieties must be obtained locally.

1 banana blossom
1 tablespoon salt
water
1 clove garlic

1 small onion
1 tablespoon corn oil
1 cup coconut milk

Remove the outer leaves and cut the blossom into quarters. Add the salt to enough water to cover the blossom and soak for 20 minutes. Drain well. Peel and crush the garlic, peel and slice the onion, and fry together in the oil until the mixture turns yellow. Add the banana blossom and coconut milk and bring the mixture to the boiling point. Serve as an accompaniment to a main meal.

BANANA BLOSSOM WITH SHRIMPS

2 banana blossoms
2 tablespoons salt
2 cups unshelled shrimps
2 cups water
2 tablespoons vinegar

1 onion
4 cloves of garlic
4 tablespoons lard
salt and pepper

Remove the outer leaves of the blossom, slice it thinly and rinse it in cold water. Sprinkle the salt over the banana blossom and work it in, squeezing by hand. Rinse in cold water and drain. Shell the shrimps and squeeze the heads. Boil the shells and heads of the shrimps for 2 minutes in the water. Drain, saving the shrimp liquor. Mix the vinegar with the peeled shrimps. Slice the onion. Peel and chop the garlic. Mix them and fry lightly in the lard. Add the peeled shrimps and the shrimp liquor to the onion mixture and bring to the boil. Add the banana blossom and cook, stirring constantly, until it is tender. Season according to taste and serve the dish hot.

BANANA CAKE

3 ripe bananas
100 g + 1 dessertspoon (4 oz)
    butter or margarine
150 g + 1½ dessertspoons (6 oz)
    white sugar
1 egg

2 tablespoons milk
225 g (8 oz) flour
1 teaspoon baking powder
1 teaspoon soda
1 teaspoon vanilla essence

Cream the butter, mix in the sugar and beat in the egg. Mash the bananas in the milk and mix them with the creamed ingredients. Sieve the flour. Add the baking powder and the soda, and combine the dry ingredients with the sugar mixture. Add the vanilla essence. Pour the batter into a lined cake tin 17-20 cm (7-8 in) and bake for 1 hour at 160°C (325°F), Gas Mark 3.

BANANA BISCUITS

3 ripe bananas
325 g + 2 dessertspoons (12 oz) flour
2 teaspoons baking powder
½ teaspoon soda
a pinch of salt
250 g + ½ dessertspoon (9 oz)
    white sugar

75 g + ½ dessertspoon (3 oz) butter
    or margarine
2 eggs
1 teaspoon vanilla essence
1 tablespoon sugar
¼ teaspoon cinnamon

Sift the flour, baking powder, soda and salt together into a mixing bowl. Stir in the first quantity of sugar and then rub the butter into the dry ingredients. Beat in the eggs. Peel and mash the bananas, and add them to the flour mixture. Beat in the vanilla, mixing well. Drop the dough by the teaspoonful on to greased paper on baking tray at 4 cm (1½ in) intervals. Mix together the cinnamon and tablespoon of sugar and sprinkle the mixture over the biscuits. Bake for 12 minutes at 200°C (400°F), Gas Mark 6. Cool and store in an air-tight container.

CHOCOLATE-COVERED BANANAS

570 ml (1 pint) water
1 teaspoon ascorbic acid

12 to 18 firm-fleshed, ripe bananas
450 g (1 lb) cooking chocolate

Boil the water, add the ascorbic acid, then cool and chill. Peel the bananas and dip them in the ascorbic acid solution. Insert cocktail sticks lengthways in each banana. Freeze the bananas on an aluminium tray. Place the chocolate in a pan and melt it over hot water at 27°C (80°F or hand warm), heating gently. Dip and twist the frozen bananas in the chocolate until they are completely covered. Hold them over the pan to drip until the chocolate hardens. Place them on waxed paper and remove the cocktail sticks. Wrap each banana in tin foil and store in the coldest part of the refrigerator. Alternatively store them in cartons in the freezer. If stored this way, allow the bananas to defrost for 10 to 15 minutes before serving.

BANANA CHUTNEY

1 kg (2 lb) peeled ripe bananas
55 g (2 oz) cloves of garlic
55 g (2 oz) red chillies
450 g (1 lb) raisins

4½ l (8 pints) vinegar
450 g (1 lb) brown sugar
170 g (6 oz) salt
225 g (½ lb) ground ginger

Slice the bananas into a preserving pan. Peel and chop the garlic and add it with the chillies, raisins and vinegar to the fruit. Simmer the mixture until the chillies and raisins are soft. Add the brown sugar, salt and ginger and boil the mixture rapidly for 10 minutes. Bottle in sterile jars while still hot.

BANANA JAM (1)

1 kg (2 lb) peeled ripe bananas
2 lemons

800 g (1¾ lb) white sugar
water

Slice the bananas into a preserving pan and add water as needed. Grate the rinds of the lemons and add it to the bananas. Squeeze the juice of the lemons on to the bananas. Add the sugar to the fruit mixture and boil rapidly until the jam is dark red. Bottle in sterile jars.

BANANA JAM (2)

12 lemons
1 cup water

12 acid Lady's Finger type bananas
white sugar

Squeeze the lemons and pour the juice into a preserving pan; add the water. Slice the bananas and add them to the pan. Measure the volume of the mixture. Bring to the boil. Add an equal amount of white sugar to the fruit and boil, with frequent stirring, until the mixture turns red. Bottle in sterile jars.

3 Brazilian Cherry *Eugenia uniflora*

Other names that may be used:

Other botanical names: Eugenia brasiliensis, Eugenia dombeya, Eugenia michelii
Other English: Cayenne cherry, Florida cherry, pitanga, Surinam cherry
French: cerise carré; cerise de Cayenne, cerise du pays (French Guiana)
Indian subcontinent languages: goraka-jambu (Singalese)
Portuguese: pitanga, pitanga do Norte
Southeast Asian languages: chermai belanda, petanga, petangi (Malaysian); ma-yom-farang (Thai)
Spanish: cereza cuadrada; cereza de Cayena

Where it grows
A few of these shrubs are grown throughout the tropics and subtropics, but they are more commonly found in the Americas than in Africa or Asia.

23

Description

It is an evergreen that may achieve a height of 7 m (23 ft) at maturity. Young leaves are a rich, wine colour, while the older leaves are small and dark green. The flowers are small, creamy-white and slightly fragrant.

The fruits, like cherries, hang singly or in small clusters on long, slender stems. They are small, thin-skinned, ribbed and flattened at the ends and different varieties can be bright cerise, dark red or nearly black in colour. They contain one or more seeds. When the fruit is ripe the flesh is soft and juicy and has a pleasant, sweet to sub-acid, aromatic, resinous flavour.

Origin and history

The Brazilian Cherry is a native of Brazil and was spread around the world by the Portuguese.

Notes on cultivation

This shrub will grow on almost any soil, even under rather dry conditions. It is usually propagated from seed but it can be grafted easily. Fruiting shrubs should be planted 3 to 4 m (10 to 13 ft) apart, but when used as a hedge plant it is, of course, planted much closer. It withstands very heavy pruning, growing slowly and becoming both dense and compact. Brazilian Cherry shrubs mature at three to five years of age but may fruit after the second year.

General uses and recipes

The ripe fruit is rich in vitamin C, but is more useful as an ingredient of recipes than as a dessert fruit.

BRAZILIAN CHERRY COMPOTE

1 cup stoned ripe Brazilian cherries   1 cup granulated sugar

Mix the fruit with the sugar and freeze. Serve with cream or ice-cream.

BRAZILIAN CHERRY ICE

1½ kg (3 lb) ripe Brazilian cherries   140 ml (¼ pint) water
white sugar

Remove the stones and squeeze the cherries to a pulp. There should be approximately 1 kg (2 lb) of pulp. Pour the water over the fruit, mix in the sugar to taste and freeze in an ice-cube tray.

BRAZILIAN CHERRY JAM

ripe Brazilian cherries   preserving sugar

Remove the stones and squeeze the cherries to a pulp. Retain the stones (for Brazilian Cherry Mould). Measure the volume of pulp. To every 3 cups of pulp, use 4 cups of sugar. Warm the sugar in a preserving pan. Add the pulp and boil quickly after the sugar has melted, until the mixture thickens. Remove the scum and retain. Store the jam in sterile jars.

BRAZILIAN CHERRY MOULD

cherry stones and scum retained from   white sugar
    making Brazilian Cherry Jam   arrowroot
water

Place the stones and the scum in a preserving pan and cover with water. Boil until the flavour is extracted. Drain and measure the liquor. To each 570 ml (1 pint) of liquor, add 2 tablespoons of white sugar. Dissolve 1½ tablespoons of arrowroot in 1 tablespoon of water. Boil the sugared liquor and the arrowroot together until the mixture thickens, stirring all the time. Set in a mould. Turn it on to a dish before serving.

4 *Breadfruit* *Artocarpus communis*

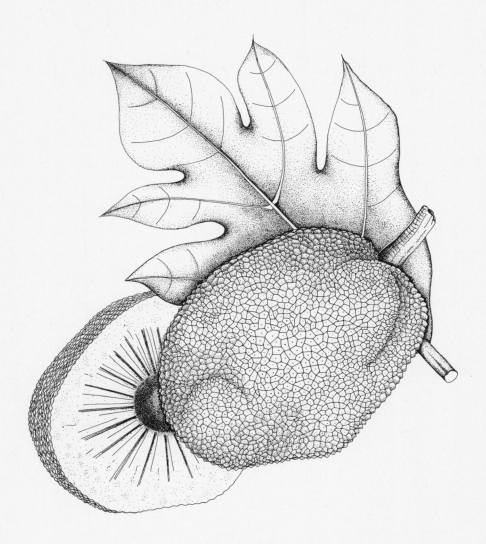

Other names that may be used

Other botanical names: Artocarpus altilis, Artocarpus incisa, Sitodium altile,
    Radermachia incisa
Dutch: broodvrucht
Other English: breadnut
French: arbe à pain

Indian subcontinent languages: erapillakai (Tamil); rata-del (Singalese)
Pacific languages: uto, kula (Fijian)
Portuguese: fruta pao (Brazil)
Southeast Asian languages: kulur, sukun (Malaysian); rimas (Tagalog); sa-ke (Thai)
Spanish: fruta de pan; pande pobre; pana cimarrona (Colombia); pana (Puerto Rico)
West African languages: am-bere-fut; barafuta (Hausa); belefu, pu-niki (Mende); blefo-akate (Krobo); bred-fut, bred-nut (Creole); dua bayere (Twi); ma-kant-ma-potho (Temne); ukwa (Ibo); yevuzi (Ewe)

Where it grows
Breadfruit thrives in the hot, humid lowland tropics below 500 to 700 m (1600 to 2300 ft) altitude and where the rainfall is 1500 to 2500 mm (60 to 100 in) per annum. It is now widely distributed in the oceanic tropics, particularly in the Pacific Islands and in the Caribbean.

Description
This is a rather handsome, quick-maturing tree, with a straight trunk and dense foliage consisting of large, leathery, lobed leaves crowded at the end of the branches. It can grow 20 to 30 m (60 to 98 ft) high.

The male flowers form a drooping club-shaped yellow or greenish-yellow spike, 15 to 30 cm (6 to 12 in) long and 2½ cm (1 in) thick. The female flowers are crowded together in large, rounded, green heads.

Fruits are borne in twos and threes at the end of branches. They may be 20 to 30 cm (8 to 12 in) in diameter, more or less round in shape, with a thick, rough, yet waxy, skin that varies from yellowish-green to brown. Inside the skin, a moist pale-yellow or whitish pulp with a mild flavour surrounds a large central core. Most varieties are seedless, but if seeds are present they are about 2½ cm (1 in) long.

Origin and history
The breadfruit was a native of Polynesia, but it had been spread by man into Southeast Asia before Europeans first visited the Pacific.

It is probable that more people now know something of the origin and history of the spread of breadfruit than have ever eaten it, since indirectly it was the cause of the most celebrated of all mutinies at sea — the mutiny on H.M.S. *Bounty* — of an epic voyage, and of the founding of a small colony of Europeans and Polynesians on the remote Pacific Island of Pitcairn.

Early European explorers in the Pacific having extolled the merits of the breadfruit as a cheap food, planters in the Caribbean islands petitioned George III to agree to the organization of an expedition to collect breadfruit trees in the Pacific and to bring them back to the Caribbean. It was believed that this tree would provide an inexpensive and easily-grown source of food for slave labour on the plantations.

The petition was granted and in 1787 *H.M.S. Bounty*, under Captain Bligh, sailed for Tahiti. The *Bounty* arrived in Tahiti on 26 October 1788 and 1,015 small breadfruit trees were collected and stored aboard. The ship sailed on 4 April 1789, but owing partly to the harsh discipline of Captain Bligh, a mutiny led by Fletcher Christian broke out on 28 April. Most of the breadfruit trees were thrown overboard and Captain Bligh, together with 18 loyalists, was set adrift in a small open boat. The mutiny spawned an extraordinary voyage as Captain Bligh navigated his small boat across 3,618 nautical miles, landing on the island of Timor in what is now Indonesia on 14 June 1789. Meanwhile the mutineers, looking for a refuge, landed at the remote island of Pitcairn and founded a Polynesian-European colony.

A second mission to secure breadfruit trees, organized in 1792, was more successful and trees from Tahiti were first planted in the islands of St Vincent and Jamaica in 1793. Breadfruit trees that have grown from suckers of the original imported trees may still be seen in the botanical garden in St Vincent. At a later date breadfruit trees were imported to most humid tropical countries.

Notes on cultivation

Breadfruit trees will grow on a variety of soils, but thrive best on fertile, well-drained sandy loams. They are propagated from root suckers, from seed or by budding and/or grafting. The young plants should be shaded.

The trees should be spaced 12 to 15 m (40 to 50 ft) apart, and they mature in seven to eight years. The fruit ripens 60 to 90 days after the emergence of the flowers, but they do not keep very well once they are ripe. Large, mature trees can produce as many as 700 fruit per year, each weighing up to 1 kg (2 lb).

General uses and recipes

It is not only the fruit of the tree that can be used. The timber is utilized, a fibre can be derived from the bark, and the latex exuded from the trunk can be used in the caulking of boats. The fruit can be baked, boiled, roasted or fried. When it is baked it has a pleasant, somewhat nutty flavour. The seeds are also edible and they can be roasted or boiled, tasting somewhat like chestnuts. In the South Pacific Islands cooked breadfruit were traditionally preserved in pits to produce a fermented food that in the Fijian language is known as *madrai*. Breadfruit blossoms, like some types of banana blossom, are also eaten.

BAKED BREADFRUIT

1 well-ripened breadfruit with the skin flattened and partially brown

salt and pepper
butter

Wash the breadfruit. Place sufficient water in a baking tin to cover the bottom and bake the breadfruit in it whole for an hour at 180°C (350°F), Gas Mark 4. When cooked, cut in half, remove the stem and core. Serve with butter, salt and pepper according to taste.

SAMOAN BAKED BREADFRUIT

1 well-ripened breadfruit
½ cup coconut cream (page 63) or butter

salt and pepper

Wash the breadfruit, put it in a baking tin containing enough water to cover the bottom, and bake at 180°C (350°F), Gas Mark 4 for an hour. After baking, scrape out and mash the flesh. Retain the half-shells. Mix the coconut cream or butter with the mashed breadfruit. Season according to taste and place the mixture in the half-shells. Reheat the shells until thoroughly hot and serve.

BREADFRUIT CHOWDER

2 thin strips of bacon
⅓ cup sliced onion
2 cups washed, peeled and chopped
   raw green breadfruit

½ cup diced carrot
2 teaspoons salt
3 cups boiling water
1⅓ cups milk

Cut the bacon into small pieces and fry until crisp. Add the onion to the bacon and fry until golden, stir in the carrot and the breadfruit. Season with salt, pour in the water, transfer the mixture to a saucepan and simmer until the vegetables become tender. Add the milk, bring to the boil and serve.

BREADFRUIT FRITTERS

1 ripe breadfruit
100 g + 2 dessertspoons (4 oz) self-
   raising flour

a pinch of salt
1 teacup water
a pan of boiling fat or oil

Wash the breadfruit. Cover the bottom of a baking tin with water, put the bread-fruit in the tin and bake it for an hour at 180°C (350°F), Gas Mark 4. Cut it in half, remove the pulp and beat it until light and frothy. Sieve the flour into a bowl and add the salt. Pour in the water gradually and beat the mixture into a smooth batter. Drop tablespoons of breadfruit pulp into the batter and fry them in the deep fat until golden.

BREADFRUIT PATTIES

1 ripe breadfruit	filling
water	grated cheese, cooked minced meat,
1 teaspoon salt	curried meat or chicken pieces
pepper to taste	boiling fat or oil for deep frying
butter to taste	tomato sauce or gravy

Wash, peel and slice the breadfruit. Place it in a saucepan and cover with water; add the salt and boil until the fruit is soft. Strain. Immediately mash the fruit. Add first the pepper, then the butter and mix to a smooth dough. Roll out the dough quite thinly and cut into half-rounds, approximately 8 cm (3 in) each. Place one heaped teaspoon of the filling on the half-rounds and turn half over. Press the ends together to form a pattie. Deep fry the patties until they are golden brown. Serve hot with tomato sauce or gravy.

BREADFRUIT CHIPS

1 firm breadfruit	fat or oil for deep frying
boiling salt water	salt

Wash, peel and core the breadfruit. Parboil and drain it. Store it overnight in the refrigerator, then slice into thin chips. Deep-fry the chips and drain. Sprinkle the chips with salt according to taste while still hot.

BREADFRUIT PUDDING

1 very ripe breadfruit	½ cup white sugar
1½ cups coconut cream (page 63)	½ teaspoon salt

Wash the breadfruit, pull out the stem, cut the fruit in half and scrape the pulp out with a spoon. Measure 3 cups of pulp. Add the remaining ingredients one by one and mix. Pour into a greased baking dish and bake for an hour at 180°C (350°F), Gas Mark 4.

CANDIED BREADFRUIT BLOSSOM

1 breadfruit blossom	sugar syrup sufficient to cover chips
cold water	

Place the blossom in a bowl and cover with cold water. Leave to soak until the skin comes off easily. Peel. Place the peeled blossom in a pan. Cover with water and boil until the blossom is soft. Drain and cool. Lay the blossom on a towel and squeeze gently to remove the water. Slice into thin chips. Measure equal parts of sugar and water, and boil until the sugar dissolves and forms a syrup. Simmer the blossom chips in the syrup for 45 minutes at a low heat. Stir continuously to prevent solidifying. Drain the chips on greaseproof paper and dry them in the sun or in a cool oven.

5 Bullock's Heart *Anona reticulata*

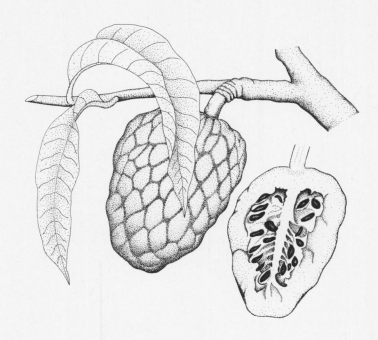

Other names that may be used

Other botanical names: Anona asiatica, Anona longifolia
The English names for various species of *Anona* are highly confusing so that
Anona reticulata and *Anona squamosa* may both be called custard apple and
sweetsop in different English-speaking communities.
Dutch: kasjoema
Other English: custard apple; sweetsop (West Indies); true custard apple
French: anone, caan, cachiman, coeur de boeuf, Corossol coeur de boeuf
Indian subcontinent languages: anoda (Singalese); ramsita (Tamil)
Pacific languages: uto ni bulumakau (Fijian)
Portuguese: araticum-apé; coração de boi (Brazil)
Southeast Asian languages: anonas, sarikaya (Tagalog); noi-noñg (Thai); lonang,
     nona kapri (Malaysian); buah nona (Indonesian)
Spanish: corazón (Colombia); anona, anona colorado (Mexico)

Where it grows
It thrives and is found everywhere in the lowland tropics and subtropics up to an
altitude of 1000 m (3300 ft), particularly where there is a seasonal climate.

Description

The bullock's heart is a shrubby tree, 4½ to 6 m (15 to 20 ft) high when mature, with a greyish, pitted bark and large (5 to 30 cm; 2 to 12 in) thin hairy leaves, shiny dark-green on the upper surface and dull pale-green on the underside. Flowers are carried on short branches and are fleshy, greenish-yellow and sweet-smelling.

The fruits are heart-shaped, buff or reddish and 8 to 13 cm (3 to 5 in) in diameter. They are borne below the leaves at the end of a thick drooping stalk. The skin of the fruit is thin but quite tough, and is covered with slightly raised, criss-cross markings. The flesh, which is creamy white and slightly granular in texture, surrounds a somewhat fibrous central core. Small black seeds are embedded in the flesh around this core. The flesh has a thick custard-like consistency and is sweet when ripe but is otherwise flavourless.

Origin and history

A native of tropical America, it was introduced to the other continents by the Portuguese. The Malaysian name of *nona kapri* is interesting as it means 'the nona from Africa', suggesting that it was probably introduced into Malaysia from Madagascar or Zanzibar and not directly from the Americas.

Notes on cultivation

It will grow in almost any soil and is normally propagated by budding or grafting; the use of seedlings is not recommended. The trees are normally spaced at 6 m (20 ft) intervals, and when mature they flower and fruit throughout the year.

General uses and recipes

The bullock's heart is used in the same way as the fruit of the other *Anona* species, but is considered inferior in quality to soursop and custard apple.

BULLOCK'S HEART DESSERT

1 ripe bullock's heart   lemon juice
sugar

Peel the fruit and squeeze the flesh through a fine sieve. Retain the juice. Add sugar and lemon juice to taste and mix them in with the juice. Serve chilled.

BULLOCK'S HEART ICE-CREAM (1)

ripe bullock's hearts   ½ cup white sugar
½ cup thick cream   1 teaspoon lemon or other citrus juice

Peel the fruit, squeeze the flesh through a fine sieve and measure out 1 cup of juice to which add the cream, sugar and citrus juice, stirring continuously. Pour the mixture into a refrigerator tray and freeze it until solid.

BULLOCK'S HEART ICE-CREAM (2)

ripe bullock's hearts
1 cup sweetened condensed milk

2 teaspoons lemon or other citrus juice

Peel the fruit, press the flesh through a fine sieve and measure out 2 cups of juice. Add the milk and citrus juice separately to the bullock's heart juice while stirring continuously. Pour the mixture into a refrigerator tray and freeze until it is solid.

BULLOCK'S HEART SHERBET

ripe bullock's hearts
4 teaspoons gelatine crystals or powder

water
170 g (6 oz) evaporated milk

Peel the fruit, squeeze the flesh through a fine sieve and measure out 1 cup of juice. Place the gelatine in a basin set over hot water in a saucepan. Pour 2 table-spoons of water over the gelatine and stir until the gelatine dissolves. Stir the bullock's heart juice into the gelatine and remove the bowl from the saucepan. Add the evaporated milk to the mixture, stir well and freeze in a refrigerator tray for an hour. Whip the mixture briskly and return it to the refrigerator until firmly set.

6 Camias *Averrhoa bilimbi*

Other names that may be used

Other English: bilimbi, bilimbing, cucumber tree, tree-sorrel
Indian subcontinent languages: bilimbikai (Tamil); biling (Singalese)
Southeast Asian languages: belimbing asam (Malaysian); belimbing wuhuh
    (Indonesian); kamias (Tagalog); ka-ling-pring, ta-ling-pring (Thai)

Where it grows
Camias is closely related to the carambola, and like that tree it grows best at
altitudes below 500 m (1600 ft) in the tropics. It is more commonly found in
Southeast Asia than elsewhere.

Description

This is a small, open tree growing up to 6 m (20 ft) tall with a short trunk, a smooth pinkish bark and small oblong leaves that grow together at the end of the twigs.

The flowers, borne on short stalks on the trunk and older branches, are small, dark red and strongly scented.

The fruits resemble small cucumbers, 7 to 10 cm (3 to 4 in) long and are produced in clusters on the trunk and the older branches. Green at first, they turn a pale yellowish colour as they ripen, when they are still very sour. Their skin is smooth and very thin, and if there are seeds they are small and are embedded in the pulp.

Origin and history

Camias is so widely grown in Indonesia and Malaysia that it is presumed to be indigenous to Southeast Asia.

Notes on cultivation

The tree thrives on well-drained sandy soil, and cultivation practises are the same as those for the carambola (page 41).

General uses and recipes

The fruit is too sour to use for desserts, but it can be pickled or preserved in syrup, makes an excellent jam and is widely used as an ingredient of chutneys and relishes. The syrup, when diluted with water and cooled, provides a delightful and refreshing drink.

The vitamin C content of this fruit is high, so high in fact that it can be used to remove stains from the hands or from white cloth.

CAMIAS PRESERVE

450 g (1 lb) firm camias fruit	680 g (1½ lb) white sugar
140 ml (¼ pint) water	8 tablespoons rosewater

Pick the stalks off the camias and prick the fruit well with a fork. Soak them in cold water for a few hours. Squeeze them by hand while they are still in the water to remove some of the acidity. Strain the fruit, wash them in hot water and dry them off. Place the water in a preserving pan, add the sugar and bring the mixture to the boil slowly. Add the prepared camias and boil, stirring constantly, for 30 minutes or until the syrup becomes thick and the fruit transparent. Add the rosewater just before taking the preserve off the heat source. Bottle and seal.

CAMIAS JAM

450 g (1 lb) firm camias fruit
680 g (1½ lb) white sugar

cinnamon to taste
water

Remove the stalks from the camias, prick the fruit well with a fork and soak them in cold water for several hours. Squeeze the fruit well, then drain off the water, wash them in hot water and dry them. Warm the sugar in a preserving pan. Add the prepared fruits to the sugar and boil gently until the jam sets. Add cinnamon if desired. Store the jam in sterile jars.

CAMIAS SAMBOL

50 small, firm camias fruit
1 tablespoon salt
570 ml (1 pint) water
12 dried chillies
1 tablespoon dried fish or shrimp
1 small red onion
3 cloves of garlic
2 small roots green ginger

5 cm (2 in) piece of cinnamon
2 2½ cm (1 in) pieces of rampa
½ stem of lemon grass
a small sprig of curry leaf
a pinch of ground saffron
1 teaspoon salt
4 tablespoons coconut oil

Cut the fruit into 5 strips lengthways. Dissolve the salt in the water. Soak the fruit in the salt solution for 30 minutes and squeeze it by hand in the water. Strain and wash the fruit under cold running water. Drain and dry the fruit on kitchen paper. Pound the chillies and the dried fish and add them to the fruit. Slice the onion and finely chop the garlic and ginger. Pound the cinnamon and add all to the fruit. Stir in the rampa, lemon grass, curry leaf, saffron and salt. Heat the oil in a preserving pan and fry all the ingredients together until the fruit is cooked. Store it in sterile jars, and serve with rice dishes.

7 Cape Gooseberry *Physalis peruviana*

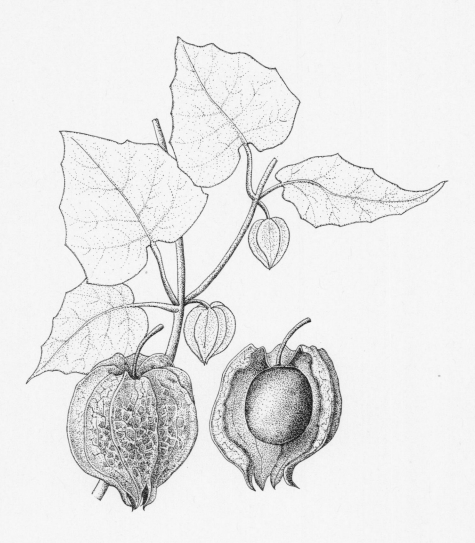

Other names that may be used

Other botanical names: Physalis edulis, Physalis esculenta
Other English: Peruvian cherry, tippari
Indian subcontinent languages: tepari; tiparee; rasbhari
Pacific languages: botebote yadra (Fijian)
Spanish: cereza del Peru (Mexico); topo-topo (Venezuela); uvilla (Ecuador)

Where it grows

The Cape gooseberry grows best in the subtropics and at medium altitude, 610 to 1830 m (2000 to 6000 ft) in the tropics. It is cultivated in the highland areas of tropical America and in Mexico, while in some parts of Africa where it has been introduced, it grows so well that it has become a weed.

Description

It is a low, straggling, herbaceous perennial plant. The flowers are bright yellow and the fruits, the size of small cherries, are covered with pale yellowish-greenish bracts, so that they look like a series of miniature Japanese lanterns. When they are quite ripe, the fruits have an agreeable and refreshing flavour.

Origin and history

The Cape gooseberry originates in Peru, but the common English name derives from the fact that it grows in abundance in the Cape province of the Republic of South Africa into which it was imported at the beginning of the nineteenth century. It was also imported at about the same time into the hill districts of Ceylon and India.

Notes on cultivation

Cape gooseberries thrive best on rich, sandy loam soils. Although the plant is a perennial, it is usually grown as an annual, for it becomes very straggly after the first year's crop. It is grown from seed, the planting distance should be ½ to 1 m (1½ to 3 ft), and young plants should be staked. The first crop of fruit can be harvested three months after planting.

General uses and recipes

The fruit can be eaten raw or cooked and can be made into delicious jam or jelly.

STEWED CAPE GOOSEBERRIES

450 g (1 lb) ripe Cape gooseberries
water

½ cup white sugar
1 pint custard

Remove the parchment material from around the berries and wash them in cold water. Add the sugar to the berries and stew them in sufficient water to cover. Allow the stewed fruit to cool. Serve with a custard or press the stewed fruit through a sieve and mix the resulting pulp with custard.

CAPE GOOSEBERRY JAM

ripe Cape gooseberries   water
preserving sugar

Take the parchment from the berries; wash them in cold water. Measure the volume. Put the berries in a preserving pan. To each cup of gooseberries, add an equal volume of sugar and of water. Boil until the jam sets when tested. Store in sterile jars.

CAPE GOOSEBERRY JELLY

ripe Cape gooseberries   white sugar
water

Remove the parchment from the berries, and wash them in cold water. Place the berries in a preserving pan and add sufficient water to cover them. Boil until the fruit is soft. Strain the fruit through a muslin bag and leave to drain overnight. Measure the volume of juice. Place the juice in a preserving pan. To each cup of juice add 4 cups of sugar. Simmer continuously, skimming off the scum until the mixture jellies. Store in sterile jars.

8 Carambola *Averrhoa carambola*

Other names that may be used

Dutch: blimbing, demaksche blimbing, fransche birambi, zoete uijfhoek
Other English: averrhoa (North America); Coramandel gooseberry (India)
French: carambole, carambolier, cornichon, pomier de Goa
Indian subcontinent languages: kamaranga (Singalese); tamarta (Tamil)
Portuguese: carambola; limas de Cayena (Brazil)
Southeast Asian languages: belimbing (Tagalog and Indonesian); belimbing manis, belimbing batu (Malaysian); ma-fu'ang, fuang (Thai)
Spanish: arbol de pepino; bilimbi; carambola; carambolera (Mexico); tiriguro (Costa Rica)

Where it grows
Carambola grows best in the lowland tropics and it is most commonly found in Southeast Asia, though it is also grown in tropical South and Central America, the West Indies, Florida, the Pacific Islands and south China.

Description

It is a moderately-sized evergreen tree with a low-branched trunk and greyish-brown or dark-grey smooth bark that grows as high as 6 to 12 m (16 to 40 ft). The leaves are dark green in colour, 3 to 18 cm (1 to 7 in) in length and are spirally arranged around the end of the twigs.

The development of small lilac-coloured flowers takes place throughout the year on panicles at the end of the branches and twigs. The fruit is a curious shape, 10 to 13 cm (4 to 5 in) long, waxy, bright golden-yellow and with five deep flutings or wings. When cut across, the section is star-shaped. The fruit is thin-skinned and fleshy with one or two seeds near to the base. The flesh is juicy, crisp and without fibre, and has an agreeably mild sweet-acid taste when it is ripe.

Origin and history

The carambola is a native of Indonesia, and possibly of Malaysia and the southern Philippines. It had spread throughout Southeast Asia and the Indian subcontinent before the advent of the Europeans, and it is probable that the Portuguese and the Spanish introduced it into the Americas from Southeast Asia.

Notes on cultivation

This tree will grow on any type of well-drained soil. It is highly wind-resistant and tolerant of dry conditions, but can be severely damaged by floods or by frost. Although usually propagated from seed, grafting is sometimes used.

Under orchard conditions, it should be planted at 7 m (23 ft) intervals and it responds to fertilizers. Carambola first fruits at five to seven years of age, and under tropical conditions it will fruit continuously with flowers, young fruit and ripe fruit always on the tree at any one time. Average yields of fruit are 45 to 136 kg (100 to 300 lb) per tree each year. There are many varieties.

The tree does not appear to suffer unduly from any major pests or diseases.

General uses and recipes

The fruit has a high vitamin-C content and good keeping quality. It can be used in fruit salads and drinks or for making jam and jelly. Because of a high ascorbic acid content, the juice can be used to remove stains, and in Southeast Asia it is used to clean brassware.

CARAMBOLA JAM

ripe carambolas   white sugar
water

Wash the fruits and cut off and discard the sharp edges. Slice the remainder into small pieces. Weigh the sliced fruit. To every 1⅛ kg (2½ lb) fruit, add 850 ml

(1½ pints) of water. Bring to the boil in a preserving pan and boil for 15 minutes. Add 1 kg (2 lb) of sugar to the pan, dissolve slowly, then boil the mixture for a further 15 minutes. When a small spoonful sets on a plate, it is done. Store in sterile jars.

CARAMBOLA JELLY

ripe carambolas   white sugar
water

Wash the fruit and cut off and discard any sharp edges. Prick the fruit all over with a fork. Place the fruit in the water in a bowl for a few hours. Squeeze the fruit by hand in the water. Drain the fruit, wash it in hot water and measure the volume of fruit retained. To each cup of prepared fruit allow 2 cups of sugar. Dissolve the sugar in sufficient water to form a thin syrup. Add the fruit and boil the mixture for 15 to 20 minutes until it begins to jell when tested. Store in sterile jars.

9 Chico *Achras sapota*

Other names that may be used

Other botanical names: Achras zapota, Manilkara achras, Manilkara zapotilla,
    Sapota achras, Sapota zapotilla
Dutch: sapodilla pruim; sapotille (Surinam); Westindische mispel
Other English: bully-tree, chikku, naseberry, neesberry, sapodilla, sapodilla-
    plum, sapota, zapote
French: nèfle d'Amerique; sapotille (French Guiana); sapotillier
Indian subcontinent languages: rata-mi (Singalese); shimai-eluppai (Tamil)
Portuguese: sapota; sapoti, sapotilha (Brazil)
Southeast Asian languages: chico (Tagalog); chicu sau Menila (Malaysian); la-mut-
    farang (Thai); sawo manila (Indonesian)
Spanish: chico; chicozapote; nispero (Colombia and Ecuador); zapotillo

Where it grows
Chico is grown almost everywhere in the lowland tropics below 1000 m (3300 ft)
altitude. In Central America and Mexico there are large commercial plantations
of the tree which is grown for the milky latex that is the source of chicle,
the main ingredient of chewing gum.

Description

The chico is a low to medium-sized tree that may grow to a height of 6 to 9 m (20 to 30 ft). It has a low-branched trunk, dark brown bark and dark green, shining, leathery leaves. The flowers are small and are borne singly, while the fruits vary in shape and size, though they are usually round or ovoid. The skin of the fruit is very thin, and when ripe it is a dullish-red or yellowish-brown colour. The pulp is pale brown, luscious and sweet, and tastes like burnt sugar. Three to as many as 12 black shining seeds are embedded in the ripe pulp.

Origin and history

This tree is a native of Central America and the West Indies, and the Spanish, after the early explorations, rapidly distributed it throughout the tropical world. It is believed that in Southeast Asia it was first taken by the Spaniards to the Philippines, and was spread from there to Malaysia. It is known to have been introduced into Ceylon around 1802.

Notes on cultivation

Chicos yield best on fertile, well-drained soils in the tropical lowlands, where there is a well-distributed seasonal rainfall. They are quite resistant to strong winds.

The majority of plantings are of seedlings, but the most desirable varieties are propagated by budding, grafting or layering. Upright varieties are planted 7 to 9 m (23 to 30 ft) spacing, while the spreading varieties require a spacing of 12 to 14 m (39 to 46 ft). The chico tree matures three to four years after planting and usually produces two crops a year. Fruiting taking place approximately four months after flowering.

General uses and recipes

The fruit is mainly used for desserts. The skin should be removed before the fruit is eaten, as it exudes a juice that is sticky and feels unpleasant on both the fingers and the lips.

Latex is obtained by tapping the trunk every two or three years. Chicle is manufactured by boiling the hardened latex. Chicle becomes plastic at mouth temperature and was used for many centuries before it was popularized in North America; it is known that it was chewed by the Aztecs and other Indian peoples. Chico trees also produce a desirable and useful timber.

CHICO PANCAKES

3 — 4 chicos	white sugar
4 heaped tablespoons plain flour	285 ml (½ pint) milk
2 eggs	oil or fat

Chico

Place the flour in a bowl and make a well in the centre. Break the eggs into the well. Mix 1 tablespoon of sugar with the eggs. Add the milk gradually, stirring all the ingredients together. Beat the resulting batter until it is smooth. Peel the chicos, remove the seeds, mash the fruit, and add it to the batter. Heat sufficient oil to cover the bottom of a frying pan. Place one spoonful of the mixture at a time into the pan and fry lightly on both sides. Sprinkle the pancakes with a little sugar and serve hot.

CHICO SWEETS

ripe chicos   castor sugar
white sugar

Cut the chicos into halves and remove the seeds. Scoop out the flesh with a spoon. Mash the fruit with a fork and measure the volume of pulp. To each cup of fruit pulp allow ⅔ cup of white sugar. Place the pulp and sugar in a preserving pan and heat until all the free water has evaporated. Spread the solid mix on a board to cool. Cut into small shapes and dry these in the sun. Sprinkle the dried sweets with castor sugar and store in air-tight jars.

10 Citrus Fruit

There are an enormous number of types of citrus fruit, and it is difficult to provide a satisfactory classification of them. They can, however, be divided into Mediterranean types (more suitable for growing in regions outside the tropics) and tropical types (that generally do not thrive very satisfactorily in cooler climates). Some varieties of both can, however, be grown in climates as varied as those of the Mediterranean and of the humid tropics.

MEDITERRANEAN TYPES

I   SWEET ORANGE   *Citrus sinensis*

Other names that may be used

Other botanical names: Citrus aurantium var. *sinensis, Aurantium sinenis, Citrus aurantium, Citrus aurantium* var. *vulgare, Citrus aurantium* var. *dulce*
Dutch: oranjeappel, sinaasappel, snif-djeroek, zoete djeroek
Other English: orange
French: orange; oranger, oranger doux, agrume
Indian subcontinent languages: naran-kai (Tamil); peni-dodan (Singalese)
Pacific languages: molidawa, molitaiti (Fijian)
Portuguese: laranja doce
Spanish: naranja
Southeast Asian languages: som kleang (Thai)
West African languages: abronkaa (Twi); akutu (Ewe); babban lemu, lemun maka (Hausa); dumbele, lumbe (Mende); lemune (Fula); ma-lemre (Temne); oloma, oloma-oyibo (Ibo); orinj (Creole); osan, osan-oyibo (Yoruba)

II   SOUR ORANGE   *Citrus aurantium*

Other names that may be used

Other botanical names: Citrus bigaradia, Citrus vulgaris
Dutch: oranjeappel
Other English: bitter orange, Seville orange
French: bigaradier, bergamotte
Pacific languages: moli jamu (Fijian)
Portuguese: laranja azêda, laranjeira azêda
Southeast Asian languages: cahel (Tagalog)
Spanish: naranja agria

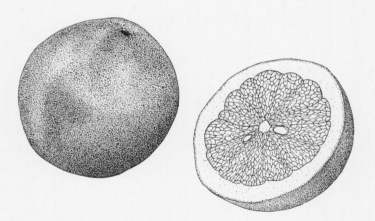

III   GRAPEFRUIT   *Citrus paradisi*

Other names that may be used

Other botanical names: Citrus decumana var. *racemosa, Citrus decumana* var.
Patoniana, Citrus maxima var. *uvacarpa, Citrus grandis*

French: pampelmousse
Portuguese: pomelo, grapefruit, cidra (Brazil)
Southeast Asian languages: buah anggur (Indonesian)
Spanish: pomelo, toronja

Crosses of the grapefruit with tangerines are known as tangelos

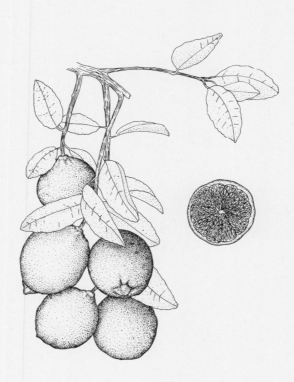

IV   LEMON   *Citrus limon*

Other names that may be used

Other botanical names: Citrus limonia, Citrus limonum, Citrus medica var. *limon,*
      Citrus medica var. *limonum, Limon vulgaris*
Dutch: citroen
French: citron, citronnier, limon
Indian subcontinent languages: kidanar-attankai (Tamil); natran (Singalese)
Pacific languages: moli karokaro (Fijian)
Portuguese: limão, limão cravo
Southeast Asian languages: ma-nao (Thai)
Spanish: limón

V CITRON

Citrus medica

Other names that may be used

Other botanical names: Citrus tuberosa, Citrus odorata, Citrus cedra, Citrus
    cedratus, Citrus crassa, Citrus fragans
Dutch: cedraat, sukadeboom
French: cédrat, cédratier
Indian subcontinent languages: cidran (Singalese)
Portuguese: cidra
Southeast Asian languages: limau susu (Malaysian); som-mu (Thai)
Spanish: cidra

IV MANDARIN   *Citrus reticulata*

Other names that may be used

Other botanical names: Citrus deliciosa, Citrus nobilis, Citrus nobilis var. *major, Citrus nobilis* var. *genuina, Citrus nobilis* var. *chrysocarpa*
Dutch: mandarijn; naartje (Republic of South Africa)
Other English: mandarin orange, tangerine
French: mandarine, mandarinier
Indian subcontinent languages: jama-naran (Singalese)
Pacific languages: moli madarini (Fijian)
Portuguese: mandarim, laranja-cravo
Southeast Asian languages: jeruk keprak (Indonesian)
Spanish: mandarina

TROPICAL TYPES

I PUMMELO   *Citrus grandis*

Other names that may be used

Other botanical names: Citrus maxima, Citrus decumana, Citrus decumanus
Dutch: pompelmoes

Citrus fruit

Other English: shaddock, pomelo, forbidden fruit
French: pampelmousse, pampelmoussier, pomme d'Adam
Indian subcontinent languages: bambalinas, jamblica (Tamil); jambola (Singalese)
Pacific languages: moli kana (Fijian)
Portuguese: toranja, laranja-melancia
Southeast Asian languages: limau Bali, limau betawi (Malaysian); ma-o, som-o
     (Thai); lukban (Tagalog)
Spanish: toronja

II   LIME   *Citrus aurantifolia*

Other names that may be used

Other botanical names: Citrus acida, Citrus limetta, Limonia aurantifolia
Dutch: limmetje
Other English: key lime, Mexican lime, sour lime
French: lime acide, limettier
Indian subcontinent languages: dehi (Singalese); dhaisi-kai (Tamil)
Pacific languages: laimi, moli laimi (Fijian)
Portuguese: lima
Southeast Asian languages: limau asam (Malaysian); ma-nao, (Thai); dayap
     (Tagalog)
Spanish: lima
West African languages: akenkaa (Twi); anguti (Ewe); kpete (Krobo); lem
     (Creole); lemo, lemu (Hausa); lemre, ma-roks (Temne); lemune-chewude
     (Fula); lumbe nyenye, lumbe-mumu (Mende); oloma, nkilisi (Ibo); orombo,
     osan (Yoruba)

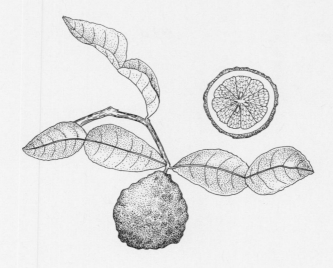

III   MAURITIUS PAPEDA   *Citrus hystrix*

Other names that may be used

Other botanical names: Citrus papeda, Papeda rumphii
Dutch: djerook poeroet
Other English: porcupine orange
French: citron combara
Southeast Asian languages: kabuyao (Tagalog); limau purut (Malaysian);
   ma-krut, som-ma-krut (Thai)

IV   KUMQUAT   *Fortunella* spp

This is not a true citrus, but many hybrids with citrus species have been produced.

Where they grow
Citrus fruits are grown from latitude 45°N to latitude 35°S, at altitudes up to
610 m (2000 ft) north and south of the tropics and up to 1830 m (6000 ft)
in the equatorial zone. Their growth is slow where the mean annual temperature
is less than 13°C (55°F) but they will withstand very high temperatures. Without
irrigation they do not thrive where the annual rainfall is less than 890 mm (35 in),
nor are they well-suited to very humid tropics. Of all citrus fruits, the mandarin
will tolerate the wettest conditions, but this fruit tree is intolerant of high winds.

53

Citrus fruit

Description

As most citrus fruits are well known and there are numerous publications describing them, detailed descriptions are not necessary here.

Sweet Orange. This is usually a low tree, 6 to 10 m (20 to 33 ft) high when mature, with a short, low-branched, sometimes spiny trunk, and a fairly dense, rounded crown. The branches do not hang down as do those of the pummelo and grapefruit, nor are they as erect as the mandarins.

The white flowers are extremely fragrant, and the fruit are borne on robust stalks. In the tropics, oranges do not develop the typical orange skin as they ripen, but remain green; the flesh inside is usually pale orange. Outside the tropics sweet oranges mature during the cooler months. Some varieties of oranges have abnormal navel fruits and in others, known as blood oranges, the pulp is not orange but red or red-streaked.

Sour Orange. The trees of this species closely resemble sweet orange trees, but the fruits are brighter coloured and rougher skinned, and possess an intensely sour pulp that leaves a bitter aftertaste.

Grapefruit. It forms a medium to large spreading, low-branched tree with a crooked trunk, drooping branches and a dense crown. The leaves are smaller than those of the pummelo and usually a darker green than orange-tree leaves. The fruits are borne singly or in clusters and are round or pear-shaped. The thick skin of the fruit is a greenish-yellow or golden-yellow. There are two major types of fruit, one white fleshed and the other red or pink fleshed. The pulp has a distinctive flavour due to the presence of the bitter glucoside, naringin. In the tropics there are sometimes two crops each year.

Lemon. The lemon is a small tree, 3 to 6 m (10 to 20 ft) high when mature with numerous thorny branches and an open, irregular crown. The leaves are pale green and are fragrant when bruised. The fruit is oblong or oval, light yellow or golden and with a thick, rough peel. The segments contain a pale yellow, sour, fragrant juice. There is a wide variation in the degree of acidity of lemons, some varieties are classified as sour and others as sweet.

Citron. This plant is a small tree or a shrub and it is 2 to 3½ m (6½ to 11 ft) high at maturity. It has a short low-branched trunk and an open, irregular crown, the young branches bear long stiff spines. The flowers are large and white or yellowish-white. Fruits are varied in shape, 6 to 20 cm (2 to 8 in) long and 5 to 10 cm (2 to 4 in) in diameter, fragrant and greenish-yellow to golden-yellow. The peel is thick and white and surrounds a fragrant sour pulp that may contain many seeds.

Mandarin. There are an extraordinary number of different types of mandarin. Typically, it is a small tree, 2 to 8 m (6½ to 26 ft) in height with a crooked or straight, usually spineless trunk and a densely-leaved crown. The leaves are smaller than those of most other citrus trees, dark shining green on the top surface and a yellowish-green on the underside. The flowers are small and white. The fruits are borne on short stalks, are usually round but flattened at both ends, and have a smooth skin densely studded with sunken oil glands that are green to orange-red in colour. The peel is thin, fragrant and easily separated from the fruit segments. The orange-coloured pulp is juicy, fragrant and sweet but somewhat acid. There may be few or many seeds.

Pummelo. The tree is large, spreading and somewhat open-crowned, and attains a height at maturity of 5 to 15 m (16 to 49 ft). The young branches are densely covered with short hair and spines, the flowers are yellowish-white. The fruits are large, round or pear-shaped and yellowish-green or yellow when ripe. The skin is very thick and pithy. The pulp may be whitish or pinkish and contains a pleasing, sweetish-tasting juice.

Lime. This is a small, many-branched tree that attains a height of approximately 5 m (16 ft) at maturity. The branches are covered with short spines. The small, yellowish-white flowers are tinged with purple along their margins. The fruits are small, round or oval with a smooth skin; very dark green when unripe, they gradually lighten as they ripen. The peel is thin and bitter, and the pulp is green to yellowish-green, very acid and fragrant. In the tropics, limes fruit all the year round.

Mauritius papeda. This forms a small tree, 2 to 12 m (6½ to 39 ft) high with a low-branched trunk and an irregular, dense crown. The leaves are of medium size and the flowers are a reddish-tinted white. Fruits are about the same size as mandarins, with a yellowish-green and very rough skin, a thick peel and a sour yellowish-green pulp.

Kumquat. This relative of the citrus is an open shrubby tree that produces small green or orange round or oval fruits. The skin of the fruit is smooth and edible. Kumquat juice is possibly the most delectable of all citrus fruit juices.

Origin and history

Sweet Orange. This species of citrus was probably indigenous to south China and Indo-China, and was cultivated there at a very early date, as it is mentioned in Chinese writing around 2200 B.C. It was probably introduced into the Mediterranean region some 2000 years later, becoming well established by the fourteenth century. Portuguese explorers introduced new and improved varieties to southern Europe from India and Southeast Asia in the fifteenth and early sixteenth centuries. Columbus planted seeds in Santo Domingo in 1493 and, after this date, cultivation of sweet oranges spread rapidly in the Americas, wild groves being recorded in St Augustine, Florida, as early as 1556.

Sour Orange. Arab traders are thought to have introduced this species into southern Europe from Southeast Asia.

Grapefruit. This species probably originated in the West Indies. The first seedless grapefruit was discovered in an orchard near Lakeland, Florida, around 1840.

Lemon. It is presumed that the lemon originated in Southeast Asia, probably in northern Burma. It is known that it was first introduced into western Asia by the Arabs about A.D. 1000 to 1200. The tree was introduced into Italy at the time of the Crusades. Columbus introduced it to the Americas, and the Portuguese established lemon trees in Brazil in 1540.

Citron. The citron was probably indigenous to Southeast Asia and was gradually introduced northwards into China and westwards into the Mediterranean region, where it was known as early as 300 B.C.

Mandarin. This species was originally indigenous to the Philippines and has been spread throughout the regions where citrus is now grown.

Pummelo. This fruit must have originated in Southeast Asia, possibly in Indonesia. There are indigenous varieties in most Southeast-Asian countries and in many Pacific islands. Descriptions of it were first recorded in Europe in the fourteenth century and the English name of 'shaddock' is said to be derived from the name of a sea captain who introduced it into Barbados from Malaysia.

Lime. Southeast Asia was the original home of the lime, but opinions differ as to whether it first came from northeastern India, northern Burma or Malaysia. In the eighteenth century, the cultivation of limes in the West Indies was encouraged by the British Navy who issued rations of lime juice to their sailors in order to combat scurvy, a nutritional deficiency disease that was prevalent among seamen who had to endure long voyages without access to fresh fruit or vegetables. As a consequence, British sailors came to be nick-named 'limeys', still a slightly derogatory term used for the British in Australia.

Mauritius papeda. This probably originated from Southeast Asia where it is widely cultivated.

Notes on cultivation
There are numerous books and pamphlets on the cultivation of citrus fruits available in all citrus-growing countries and the reader is advised to consult these local publications for details of cultivation.

General uses and recipes
Citrus fruits are universally used fresh for desserts, for the production of fruit juices, jams etc., and for the manufacture of a variety of other products such as essential oils (obtained from both the peel and the seeds), pectin and citrus molasses and citrus pulp (used as livestock feeds). The pulp is usually rich in vitamin C, sugars and citric acid.

Sweet oranges are used mainly fresh for desserts or for the manufacture of juice. Sour oranges are used to make marmalade. Grapefruits are used fresh for desserts, for canning and for juice. Lemons, which contain less sugar and more citric acid than oranges, are used fresh as a condiment in cooking, for the manufacture of lemonade and for juice manufacture. Candied peel is made from citron, the fruit being fermented for a month or longer in salt brine. Mandarins are eaten fresh in desserts, are canned and are used in the manufacture of juice. Pummelos are a favourite dessert fruit in Southeast Asia, but are generally unknown outside the tropics. Limes are used in the same ways as lemons. A fragrant candied peel is made from the Mauritius papeda and is used as a seasoning in cooking. Kumquats provide a particularly delicious fruit juice.

LEMON CURD

2 lemons
2 eggs

170 gm (6 oz) white sugar
55 gm (2 oz) margarine

Wash and dry the lemons. Finely grate the rind. Squeeze out the juice and remove the pips. Break the eggs into a cup. Place the sugar, margarine, eggs and lemon rind into a pan. Mix with a wooden spoon and stir over a low heat until the sugar has been dissolved and the margarine melted. Add the lemon juice and bring the mixture to the boil. Let the mixture boil slowly whilst stirring for a further 3 minutes. Seal whilst hot in sterile jars.

SPICY LEMON PICKLE

450 g (1 lb) lemons
3 tablespoons salt
115 g (4 oz) red peppers
1 clove garlic

1 teaspoon paprika
3 cups mustard oil (if this is not
    available any other vegetable
    cooking oil may be used)

Wash and dry the lemons. Cut them into quarters and place in a bowl. Sprinkle the salt over the fruit. Cover the bowl and allow it to stand for 4 days. Crush the red peppers and the garlic and add them to the lemons with the paprika. Heat the oil to boiling point and pour it over the fruit. When the mixture is cool, cover it once again and allow it to stand for 4 more days. Store the pickle in clean jars.

KUMQUAT MARMALADE

450 g (1 lb) kumquats
285 ml (½ pint) water

800 g (1¾ lb) white sugar

Wash and halve the kumquats, remove the seeds and mince the fruit. Place the minced fruit in a preserving pan. Pour the water over it and boil for 20 minutes. Stir in the sugar and boil for a further 45 minutes. Test for setting. When set, seal in sterile jars.

57

SHADDOCK MARMALADE

shaddocks	salt
water	lemon juice
white sugar	

Scrub the shaddocks well, cut each into 6 pieces and remove the centre core. Cut up the fruit into small pieces and weigh. To each 680 g (1½ lb) of prepared fruit allow 5 ⅔ l (10 pints) of water, 4½ kg (10 lb) sugar, a teaspoon of salt and 285 ml (½ pint) lemon juice. Add the water to the prepared fruit and leave the mixture over-night. On the following day boil the mixture slowly in a preserving pan for 35 minutes or until the fruit sinks to the bottom. Add the sugar, stirring until it dissolves. Add the salt and boil the mixture fast for 30 minutes. Add the lemon juice and boil for a further 30 minutes or until the marmalade sets on a spoon. Remove the marmalade from the heat source, skim off the scum and let it stand for 10 minutes before bottling in sterile jars.

THREE-FRUIT MARMALADE

2 grapefruits	3½ l (6 pints) water
4 lemons	2¾ kg (6 lb) preserving sugar
2 sweet oranges	

The total weight of the fruit should be approximately 1½ kg (3 lb). Wash all the fruit thoroughly and peel it. Slice the peel thinly. Cut up the fruit. Remove the pips and the pith and place them in a muslin bag. Soak the peel and the contents of the muslin bag in the water overnight. The next day boil the mixture in a preserving pan and then simmer gently for 1½ to 2 hours. At this stage the peel should be soft. Add the sugar to the fruit in the preserving pan and stir until it dissolves. Boil the mixture rapidly until the setting point is reached. Skim off the froth. Bottle the marmalade in sterile jars.

CANDIED PEEL

peel from 3 oranges or lemons	preserving sugar or
1 tablespoon salt	white granulated sugar
cold water	

Scrape the pith from the peel and sprinkle the salt over the peel. Pour 4 cups of water over the peel and allow the mixture to stand overnight. The next day drain and wash the peel thoroughly. Place the peel into a preserving pan and again cover it with water. Bring to the boil and drain. Repeat this process three times. When the peel is cool cut it into thin strips and measure the volume. To each 2 cups of peel, allow 2 cups of sugar and ½ cup of water. Dissolve the sugar in the water. Add the peel and boil for approximately 30 minutes or until the peel is translucent. Drain the peel on kitchen paper and cool. Roll the peel in the sugar and dry it on a rack. Store in airtight containers.

11 Coconut *Cocos nucifera*

Other names that may be used

Dutch: calapusboom, cocos, cocosboom, cocos-palm, kalappus, klapper,
 klapperboom, klapperpalm, koko, kokosboom, kokosnootenboom,
 kokosnootpalm, kokospalm
French: cocotier, cocotier commun, cocotier des Indes, cocotier nucifere,
 cocotier ordinaire, cocotier porte-noix, palmier
Indian subcontinent languages: pol (Singalese); tennai, thenga (Tamil)
Pacific languages: niu, niu dina (Fijian)
Portuguese: côco (da Bahia)

Southeast Asian languages: kelapa, kelapa gading, nyiur (Malaysian); niog (Tagalog);
    ma-phrao (Thai)

Spanish: coco

West African languages: akwakwar, attagaro, (Hausa); ako beke, akoibo (Ibo);
    agbon (Yoruba); an-gbaro-a-potho (Temne); koknat (Creole); pu-lolui,
    kokonati (Mende); yeyu-ne, ne-ti (Ewe)

Where it grows

The coconut thrives in humid lowland, tropical areas approximately 15° longitude
north and south of the equator at altitudes below 610 m (2000 ft), where the
annual mean temperature is 25°C (77°F) or above, the rainfall is not too seasonal
and no less than 1500 mm (59 in), and on soils that possess a fluctuating but not
too high water table. They grow particularly well along the shorelines of oceanic
tropical islands and are more numerous on the Pacific and Indian Ocean shores
than on those of the Atlantic.

Description

There are three major types of palm: the tall, the dwarf and the hybrid, the last
being an intermediate type. Mature height may vary from 5 to 30 m (16 to
98 ft).

The trunk, 20 to 40 cm (8 to 16 in) in diameter, unbranched, usually slightly
thickened at the base and irregularly marked with the scars of fallen leaves, does
not increase in diameter with age. It is surmounted by a spirally-arranged,
feathery crown of leaves. The latter are large, usually 4 to 6 m (13 to 20 ft)
long and with a very robust central rib and numerous leaflets, decreasing in size
towards the tip of the leaf.

Male and female flowers emerge in sprays from the top of the palm, the
greyish-yellow male flowers first, beyond yellowish-green female flowers nearer
the base of the spray. Male flowers are far more numerous than the female ones,
and there may be as many as 8000 male to 30 female. Tall coconuts cross-
pollinate, but Malayan dwarf coconuts are self-pollinating. The nuts take approximately 18 months to mature and one flowering stalk emerges every month,
so that in an equatorial climate the production of mature nuts is continuous.

Nuts vary in colour, size and shape. Tall trees produce orange or green nuts,
the Fijian dwarf variety green ones and the Malayan dwarf variety orange or
yellow ones. Beneath the smooth outer skin is a thick layer of fibrous husk. The
nut itself is hard-shelled, but at one end are three sunken 'eyes' of softer tissue,
from one of which the shoot and root emerge when the nut germinates. Inside
the hard shell there is a thin, white, fleshy layer known as coconut meat, while
the hollow interior is partially filled with a sweet watery liquor known as
coconut water. The volume of coconut water is greatest while the nut is still
unripe.

Origin and history

There are no wild coconuts, and it is not known for certain where the coconut originated, but it was probably somewhere in the Pacific Ocean or in the Malay Archipelago. The nut is exceedingly well adapted to travel and remains fertile in salt water, so coconuts have probably distributed themselves throughout the Pacific and Indian Ocean regions. The early Spanish explorers found them growing on the Pacific coast of tropical America but not along the Atlantic coast, save on the Isthmus of Panama. It is believed that they were imported to the Atlantic coast of Panama by the indigenous inhabitants of the isthmus, who presumably obtained them from the nearby Pacific coast. Coconuts were introduced into the West Indies in 1525, being imported from the Cape Verde Islands to Puerto Rico.

Notes on cultivation

The coconut will grow on any well-drained soil as long as its other environmental requirements are satisfied, but it thrives best on deep alluvial soils with a fluctuating water table. It is propagated from seed, as vegetative propagation is not yet possible. Selected nuts are laid on their long side and partially covered by soil in a nursery area. The soil should cover one-half to two-thirds of the nut. Germination occurs after about two months and within six months the young nuts are ready for transplanting.

Tall palms are spaced at 9m² (30 ft²), while the dwarf varieties are spaced at 6 to 7m² (20 to 24 ft²). At first the tree does not appear to grow as the growing point develops, then the trunk slowly emerges. The tall varieties first fruit from the sixth to the ninth year; full fruiting is achieved at the twentieth year and fruiting continues for up to 80 years. The dwarf varieties first fruit at four to five years of age and full fruiting commences when the palm is eight years old. Coconuts respond well to fertilization and in particular to fertilizers with a high potash content.

Tall trees produce on average 50 nuts per year, while the dwarf trees will produce up to 100 much smaller nuts. Land between coconuts can be inter-cropped and coconut production can be combined with livestock raising if pasture is planted under the trees.

Nuts used for cooking should be picked before they are ripe and drop to the ground.

As coconuts are propagated from seed there are many varieties. For example, in the Fiji Islands the following varieties are utilized. *Niu vula* — a tall palm with green nuts; *nui dama* — a tall palm with orange nuts; *niu drau* — a tall palm bearing a large number of small green nuts; *niu ni toga* — a tall palm bearing large nuts; *niu ni nagimagi* — a tall palm bearing elongated nuts with a high proportion of husk; *rotuman* — a tall palm bearing a small number of very large nuts; *niu yabia* — a tall 'weeping' coconut that bears a small number of nuts; *niu leka* —

the Fijian dwarf palm that bears green nuts; together with introduced varieties such as the Malayan dwarf.

General uses and recipes

The coconut is an exceptionally useful plant. Trunks may be used in house building, for short-lived fence posts or for building bridges. The leaves are suitable for thatch or for building the walls of houses. Coir, obtained from the husk by retting, is used for making ropes, mats, brooms etc.

Water in the green immature nuts is used either fresh or iced as a refreshing drink, while the immature flesh can be scooped out of the shell and eaten. Mature flesh can be eaten fresh, dried and used (as desiccated coconut) in confectionary, dried to produce copra, or grated to produce coconut 'cream' (a major ingredient used in the cooking of meat, fish and vegetables in the Pacific Islands and in Southeast Asia). Copra, when pressed or extracted with solvents, produces coconut oil and coconut cake. Coconut oil can be used for cooking or in the manufacture of soap, and coconut cake is an excellent livestock concentrate feed.

Sap, collected by cutting the tip of the unopened flowering shoot, is a source of sugar as it contains up to 16 per cent sucrose. It can be used to provide a delightful fresh drink or can be fermented to form an alcoholic drink known as toddy. The latter can be distilled to produce a strong alcoholic spirit.

Shells can be turned into drinking utensils, buttons, curios or a high-quality charcoal.

The growing bud of the palm provides a delicious white, crisp salad with a nutty flavour. As the tree is killed by the removal of the growing bud this is probably the most expensive salad in the world and indeed in the South Pacific it is known as 'millionaire's salad'.

Normal tall palms sometimes produce abnormal nuts whose centre is completely filled with a firm spongy mass. This is known as *makapuno* in the Philippines and these nuts are highly prized, fetching up to ten times the value of ordinary nuts in the market. They are used in the manufacture of highly-priced confectionary.

COCONUT CREAM AND/OR COCONUT MILK

1 ripe coconut   2 teacups hot water

Crack the nut in half crossways and grate the white flesh. This is best done on a specially made grater consisting of an iron claw attached to a board or to a wooden stool. The cook sits astride the stool and grates the half coconuts on the iron claw. It can also be done, less satisfactorily, by extracting the white flesh from the shell and putting it through a blender. Pour the hot water over the grated coconut and let the mixture stand for a few minutes, until it is possible to squeeze the mixture by hand. Strain through muslin or a sieve until all the liquid is extracted. This first extracted liquor is known as the 'cream'. The whole process may be repeated once or even twice. The second and subsequent extracted liquors are known as the 'milk'. The cream can be served with all types of desserts, hot or cold, but it should never be boiled for it will curdle. The milk is used in cooking meat, fish and vegetables.

GREEN COCONUT DRINK

1 green coconut

Split the nut into halves. Save and chill the coconut water. Scoop out the flesh and cut it into strips. Place the strips of flesh in a glass and pour the coconut water over it. Serve well chilled.

COCONUT SOUP

570 ml (1 pint) beef stock
½ cup barley or 1 tablespoon of
   cornflour

1 teaspoon curry powder
1 tablespoon water
1 cup coconut cream

Boil the barley in the beef stock to thicken it or mix the cornflour in a little cold water and add it to the boiling stock. Strain the soup. Mix the curry powder with the water and pour the mixture into the hot soup. Add the coconut cream just before serving the soup.

AUBERGINES BAKED IN COCONUT CREAM

4 medium aubergines
1 small onion
chillies

½ teaspoon salt
coconut cream

Wash and slice the aubergines into 2½ cm (1 in) thick rounds. Place these in a pie-dish. Peel and slice the onion; sprinkle it over the aubergines. Use 2½ chillies according to taste. Cut them up and add them to the aubergines. Season with salt. Pour enough coconut cream into the pie-dish to cover the vegetables. Bake at 180°C (350°F), Gas Mark 4 until the vegetables are tender (approximately 20 mins).

RAW FISH IN COCONUT CREAM

340 g (12 oz) any good-quality white fish
¾ cup lemon juice
2 teaspoons finely-chopped onion

1 chopped chilli
½ cup coconut cream (page 63)
salt

Skin and fillet the fish. Cut the fillets into 1¼ cm (½ in) cubes. Pour the lemon juice over the fish and leave it to soak for at least 4 hours. The lemon juice must totally cover the fish. Strain off the juice and wash the fish well in cold water. Mix the onion, chilli and coconut cream with the fish, and add salt to taste. Stand it in either the refrigerator or a cool place. Serve as a fish salad. It will keep for up to 24 hours in a refrigerator.

COCONUT OR MILLIONAIRE'S SALAD

white heart of a young coconut tree ½ onion
½ cup white vinegar mayonnaise
a pinch of salt

Wash the coconut heart, place it in a bowl, and pour the vinegar over it. Add the salt and chill the heart until it is crisp. Drain off the vinegar and shred the heart. Extract the juice from the onion and add it to the coconut heart. Serve with mayonnaise.

GREEN NUT SPECIAL

1 green coconut Vanilla ice cream

Split the nut into halves. Chill one half in a refrigerator. Scoop out the flesh of the other half and cut it into strips. Keep well chilled until ready to serve. Place a scoop of the ice-cream into the chilled half-nut, cover it with strips of the flesh and serve.

COCONUT PIE

1 green coconut ¼ cup evaporated milk
340-400 g (12-14 oz) pie pastry ⅓ cup cornstarch
¾ cup white sugar

Divide the pastry into two parts. Roll out one part to line a 20 cm (8 in) pie dish, and part-bake it. Crack the green nut; measure out ½ cup of the coconut water. Scoop out the soft flesh, measure out 2 cups of it, cut this into thin strips and place these in a pan. Add the sugar and evaporated milk. Then, stirring continuously, add the cornstarch and heat until it thickens. Pour the thickened mixture into the part-baked pastry and cover it with the remaining pastry. Bake in an oven at 200°C (400°F), Gas Mark 6 for 30 to 35 minutes.

COCONUT ICE-CREAM

1 packet fruit jelly (preferably raspberry
   or strawberry flavour)
1.1 l (2 pints) water

½ cup white sugar
570 ml (1 pint) coconut cream

Dissolve the jelly in the water in a bowl set over hot water in a saucepan or
according to instructions on the packet. Add the sugar to the dissolved jelly.
Stir the coconut cream into the jelly and freeze it.

COCONUT EGG CUSTARD

1 cup brown sugar
¼ cup water
2 cups coconut cream (page 63)
4 egg whites

6 egg yolks
1 cup white sugar
1 lemon

Place the sugar and water in a pan and cook until the sugar caramelizes. Pour
¾ of the caramel into a 2 pt Pyrex or oven-ware dish. Retain ¼ of the caramel
in the pan. Pour the coconut cream into the pan and stir until all the caramel
has dissolved. Beat the egg whites gently. Stir the yolks into the whites, then
gently stir the sugar into the eggs. Grate the rind of the lemon into the eggs and
combine all with the cream in the pan. Strain the mixture through a muslin
cloth into the dish. Stand it in a dish of hot water and bake in the oven at 180°C
(350°F), Gas Mark 4 for approx. 1½ hours. Serve when cold.

FRESH COCONUT BISCUITS

5 tablespoons butter or margarine
75 g + ½ dessertspoon white sugar
75 g + 1 dessertspoon plain flour

pinch of salt
55 g (2 oz) freshly-grated coconut

Cream the fat well and beat the sugar into it. Add the flour, salt and coconut and
mix all together. Grease a baking sheet and drop the mixture by teaspoonfuls
at 5 cm (2 in) intervals on it. Bake at 180°C (350°F), Gas Mark 4 until the biscuits
are golden brown (approximately 15 minutes). Cool. Store them in an airtight
container.

COCONUT CANDY

1½ coconuts
2 cups brown sugar
1 dessertspoon butter or margarine

1 tablespoon vinegar
   red food colouring

Crack the coconuts, grate the meat and put the grated coconut in a pan. Add the sugar, butter and vinegar to the coconut and boil together, stirring all the while, for 8 minutes. Remove the pan from the heat and beat the mixture until it thickens. Pour half the mixture on to a buttered tray. Add the red food colouring to the second half of the mixture and quickly pour it over the first half. Cut into squares before it completely cools. When the candy is set, break it into smaller pieces. Store in airtight containers.

COCONUT JAM

1 coconut   2 cups brown sugar
3 cups hot water   1 cup glucose

Extract the coconut cream and the milk 3 times as in the recipe on page 63. Mix the liquids in a preserving pan. Add the brown sugar to the mixture in the preserving pan, then the glucose. Cook over a low heat, stirring, until it thickens. Store the jam in sterile jars.

12 Custard Apple *Anona squamosa*

Other names that may be used

Other botanical names: Anona asiatica, Anona biflora, Anona cinerea, Anona
  forskahlii
Dutch: boea nona; kaneelappel (Surinam); sirikaja (Indonesia)
Other English: sugar apple (West Indies); sweetsop
French: anone écailleute, ata, attier, pomme cannelle
Pacific languages: apeli (Fijian)

Portuguese: ata; araticum-pitaiá; fruta do Conde (Brazil); pinha
Southeast Asian languages: atis, ates, yates (Tagalog); noi-na (Thai); nona seri
    kaya (Malaysia)
Spanish: anón (Colombia); anona; anona blanca (Mexico)
West African languages: brofo, nyankoma (Twi); habue (Krobo); yeru-nyikle
    (Ewe)

A cross between *Anona squamosa* and *Anona cherimolia* is known as the atemoya.

Where it grows

Custard apples thrive almost everywhere in the lowland tropics. They tolerate colder weather and drier conditions than either the soursop or the bullock's heart.

Description

The custard apple is a small tree, 4½ to 6 m (15 to 20 ft) high with irregular spreading branches and a greyish-brown bark. All parts of the tree emit a distinctive odour when broken or bruised.

The leaves are oblong, 5 to 17 cm (2 to 7 in) in length and are coloured medium to pale green on top and bluish-white on the under surface. The solitary, small flowers are yellowish-green.

The fruits are borne on thick, woody stalks. They are more or less round, being 6 to 9 cm (2½ to 3½ in) in diameter, and usually have a pale green scaled skin covered with a waxy, greyish bloom when ripe. There are some purple-fruited varieties. When the fruit is ripe the flesh is white and custard like, with a delightful aroma and a very sweet, agreeable flavour. It often falls into segments in the hand. There may be up to 80 black, shiny seeds, loosely embedded in the ripe flesh.

Origin and history

The custard apple is indigenous to tropical America. It appears to have been introduced into Asia soon after the first European voyage to the Americas, as it was already cultivated in Indonesia when the Dutch arrived. It was probably imported into the Philippines by the Spanish and into India, Indonesia and Malaysia by the Portuguese.

Notes on cultivation

This tree thrives best on light, sandy soils in a tropical climate where there is a definite dry season. It is frequently raised from seed, but superior varieties are propagated vegetatively by budding or grafting. The recommended planting distance is 6 m (20 ft). Custard apple trees mature early and first fruit when they are three to five years old. It is not very easy to harvest the fruits, as when they are ripe and fit to pick, they tend to burst open on the tree.

69

General uses and recipes

The fruit has a high mineral content and may be eaten fresh or chilled, or used as a base for fruit salads, fruit cups, ice cream and sherbert. It is not as strongly flavoured as the soursop, and other flavourings such as peppermint or ginger may be added to introduce variety. Green or other food colourings are also sometimes added to the pulp.

CUSTARD APPLE DESSERT

The recipe is the same as that for Bullock's Heart Dessert (page 33), substituting custard apples for the bullock's heart.

CUSTARD APPLE ICE-CREAM (1)

The recipe is the same as that for Bullock's Heart Ice-Cream (1) (page 33), substituting custard apples for the bullock's heart.

CUSTARD APPLE ICE-CREAM (2)

The recipe is the same as that for Bullock's Heart Ice-Cream (2) (page 34). substituting custard apples for the bullock's heart.

CUSTARD APPLE ICE-CREAM (3)

To make 4½ l (1 gallon) of ice-cream:

8 to 12 medium, ripe custard apples	4 340 g (12 oz) cans evaporated milk
½ cup cold water	1 340 g (12 oz) can condensed milk
white sugar	

Remove the seeds and crush the fruit. Strain, adding a small volume of water so that all the juice can be squeezed out. Mix the evaporated and condensed milks in an ice-cream freezer. (This recipe can also be made in the refrigerator or any ice-cream maker) Add the juice and sugar to taste, and stir until the sugar has dissolved. Shut the ice-cream freezer and turn the crank until the mixture hardens. Transfer the ice-cream to a suitable container and place this in the freezer for final freezing. If a freezer is not available, continue to crank the ice-cream freezer until the mixture is properly frozen. Serve.

CUSTARD APPLE SHERBET

This recipe is the same as that for Bullock's Heart Sherbet (page 34), substituting custard apple for the bullock's heart.

13 Durian *Durio zibethinus*

Other names that may be used

Dutch: doerian, doorian, stinkvrucht
Other English: civet-cat tree, civet-fruit
French: dourian, durion, durione
Southeast Asian languages: rian, durian (Malaysian and Indonesian); thu-rian (Thai)

Where it grows
The durian tree is found mainly in the humid tropical areas of Southeast Asia at altitudes below 800 m (2600 ft). The tree is hardly known in tropical America but is grown on the east coast of Africa, particularly in Zanzibar.

Description
The tree is large and lofty, growing as high as 30 m (100 ft), with a straight trunk, irregular and dense foliage and a tough, dark-grey flaky bark.

The leaves are large, 6 to 25 cm (2 to 10 in), and green on the top surface, light golden-yellow below. The large evil-smelling, yellowish-white flowers hang in masses on pendulous branches.

Fruits vary in size and shape but generally they are large, weighing 2 to

4½ kg (4½ to 10 lb), dull yellow when ripe and covered in spines. The outer shell of the fruit is woody, but inside a rich, creamy, yellowish-white pulp surrounds two to six brown seeds that are about the size of large chestnuts. The fruit falls when it is ripe, and the quality rapidly deteriorates once it has matured.

Origin and history
Durian is indigenous to several Southeast Asian countries, including the Philippines, Indonesia, Malaysia and Thailand.

Notes on cultivation
The tree appears to grow on any fertile soil. It has been propagated by seed in the past, but new improved varieties are propagated by budding. It should be spaced at 14 m (40 ft) intervals, and first fruits at about seven years after planting.

General uses and recipes

Durians have a peculiarly strong, offensive odour that permeates the refrigerator, a room or the market place. As a consequence, in most Southeast Asian countries, airlines refuse to allow passengers to carry it in their hand luggage. The taste is another matter. Those unaccustomed to it are inclined to believe that it must be unpleasing, but *aficionados* are passionately addicted. The edible pulp is so delicious that the best variety in Thailand has been described as 'something like honey but it melts in your mouth like butter' and the more you eat the less inclination you have to stop. It is said in Indonesia that elephants will travel long distances to find ripe fruit and that tigers relish it.

The fresh pulp can be frozen and thawed whenever it is required, made into jam, candied, or used in the manufacture of sweets and cakes. In Indonesia the pulp is fermented, when it is known as *tempoya*. This may be mixed with rice and sugar to make *tempong* or with salt, vinegar and onions to form *boder*. The large seeds can be roasted and eaten.

DURIAN CAKE

1 ripe durian	4 eggs
150 g + 1½ dessertspoons (6 oz) butter	150 g + 3 dessertspoons (6 oz) plain flour
125 g + 1 dessertspoon (5 oz) white sugar	

Remove the pulp from the outer flesh of the durian. Cut the pulp, remove the seeds and crush the pulp. Weigh out 100 g and 1 dessertspoon (4 oz) of the pulp. Place the butter and the sugar in a mixing bowl and cream them together.

Separate the eggs. Beat the yolks into the butter-sugar mixture. Save the whites. Beat the weighed pulp into the creamed mixture. Whisk the egg whites stiff and fold them into the mixture. Add the flour and stir it in gently. Pour the mixture in to a greased cake tin and bake for one hour at 180°C (350°F), Gas Mark 4.

DURIAN CANDY

1 ripe durian   white sugar

Remove the pulp from the durian's outer flesh. Cut the pulp, remove the seeds, crush the pulp and measure 1 cup of it. Add half a cup of sugar to the durian pulp in a pan. Cook over medium heat until the mixture thickens sufficiently to be formed into balls. Transfer the cooked, thickened mixture to a board dusted with sugar and roll it out until ½ cm (¼ in) thick. Slice with a sharp knife to make sweets of the desired size and wrap each in waxed paper or cellophane.

DURIAN JAM

1 ripe durian   ½ cup white sugar
1 tablespoon of water   lemon juice (optional)

Remove the pulp from the outer flesh. Cut the pulp, remove the seeds, crush pulp and measure 1 cup of it. Place the pulp in a pan. Add a little water and bring it slowly to the boil. Add the sugar and stir. If desired, add a little lemon juice. Boil the mixture rapidly, stirring continuously, until it reaches setting consistency. Remove the jam from the heat, but continue stirring for 5 minutes more to keep the fruit from rising to the top. Stir gently to prevent the formation of air bubbles. Pack the jam in hot sterile jars. Store the jam in a dry, cool and dark place, as this helps it to retain its colour and flavour.

14 *Granadilla* *Passiflora quadrangularis*

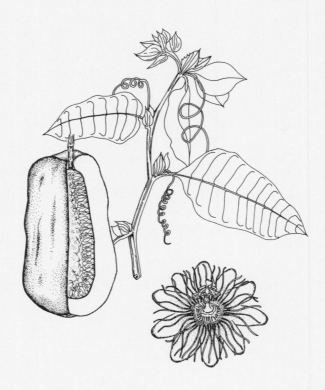

Other names that may be used

Dutch: djari markoesa; groote markoesa (Surinam); markiza
Other English: common granadilla, giant granadilla, grenadilla, square-stalked
   passion fruit
French: barbadine
Indian subcontinent languages: rata-puhul (Singalese); seemaisora-kai (Tamil)
Portuguese: maracujá-assu; maracujá mamâo; maracujá melâo (Brazil); peroba
Southeast Asian languages: markisah (Indonesian); marquesa, timun belanda
   (Malaysian); sukhontha-rot (Thai)
Spanish: granadilla real (Costa Rica); parcha de Guinea, parcha granadina
   (Venezuela); pasionaria (Cuba); tumbo (Ecuador)

Where it grows
This vine is common throughout the lowland, warm, humid oceanic tropics.
It does not thrive at medium to higher altitudes.

Description

The granadilla is a vine with a yellowish-green, thick, square stem that grows
5 to 50 m (16 to 164 ft) and possesses robust tendrils 22 to 35 cm (9 to 14 in)
long. Its leaves are large, 10 to 25 cm (4 to 10 in) long and 8 to 17 cm (3 to 7 in)
wide, elliptical in shape and with a dark, shining-green surface and a light green
or yellowish-green underside.

Granadilla flowers are of the passion-flower type, 25 to 30 cm (10 to 12 in)
in diameter, fragrant, showy and attractive. They are borne on single, short stalks.

The fruit is the largest of all passion fruits and varies in shape, being
normally 15 to 25 cm (6 to 10 in) long and 10 to 15 cm (4 to 6 in) in diameter.
The skin is thick and white or yellowish-white, with a rather insipid taste. The
pulp consists of hard, flat seeds, each surrounded by gelatinous material, and is
juicy, somewhat sweetish and slightly acid in taste and white or yellowish-white
in colour. The seeds have a slightly acid flavour.

Origin and history

This vine is a native of tropical America and was first cultivated in the eighteenth
century.

Notes on cultivation

Granadillas thrive on well-drained sandy loam soils. They are propagated by seeds,
by layering or by cuttings taken from the mature wood. The vine requires support
and should be spaced at 2 to 3 m (6½ to 10 ft) intervals. The flowers are
pollinated by specific insects, but hand-pollination is recommended to ensure
successful fruiting.

The vines first fruit at six months of age and last for five to six years, after
which replanting should be practised.

General uses and recipes

Unripe, the fruit may be cooked as a vegetable. The rind of the ripe fruit can
be used separately as a vegetable or as a substitute for apple pulp. The pulp
with the seeds included can be added to fruit salads or used to make a refreshing
drink.

GRANADILLA ICE

1 ripe granadilla	1 wine glass brandy or port
450 g (1 lb) white sugar	a pinch of salt
water	

Cut the granadilla into halves lengthways. Scoop out the pulpy seeds into a bowl.
Remove the tough inner skin. Scrape the flesh off the outer part of the fruit

with a spoon and add it to the seeds. Add the sugar, brandy and salt to the fruit. Measure the volume of the mixture. Make up the mixture to a total volume of 1½ litres (3 pints) with water. Mix well and freeze.

GRANADILLA DRINK

1 ripe granadilla   sugar

Cut the granadilla in half lengthways. Place the pulp and the seeds in a bowl, mash with a fork or mix in a blender and strain out the juice. Add sugar to the juice according to taste. Serve chilled.

GRANADILLA SAVOURY

1 green, firm granadilla   salt
water   butter or white sauce

Peel the granadilla, remove the seeds and the inner skin, and cut the remainder into finger-length pieces. Place the fruit in a pan and just cover it with water. Add salt to taste. Boil the fruit quickly until tender. Drain, serve with butter or white sauce.

MOCK APPLE

1 green, firm granadilla   ½ cup water approximately
sugar   butter
¼ cup lemon juice

Peel the granadilla and remove the seeds and inner skin, cut up the remainder and place it in a pan. Add sugar to taste, with the lemon juice and a little water. Cook until the fruit softens. Remove from the heat and mash the fruit with a fork. Beat a small knob of butter into the fruit. Serve it as you would apple sauce.

GRANADILLA CHUTNEY

green firm granadillas   brown sugar
salted water   medium onions
small chillies   vinegar
cloves   salt
cinnamon

Peel and halve the granadillas, scoop out the seeds and save them. Discard the inner skin of the granadillas and cut up the green outer part of the fruit. Parboil this in salted water. Drain it and measure the volume of fruit. For each 4 cups of fruit, allow 4 chillies, 1 teaspoon each of cloves and cinnamon, 340 g (12 oz) of brown sugar, 1 onion, 850 ml (1½ pints) of vinegar and a pinch of salt. Put the chillies, cloves and cinnamon in a muslin bag with the granadilla seeds. Place the fruit, sugar and spice bag together in a preserving pan. Peel and slice the onion or onions, add to the fruit mixture and pour the vinegar over it. Season with salt. Boil until the mixture thickens (approximately one hour) remove the muslin bag and bottle the chutney in sterile jars.

15 Guava *Psidium guyava*

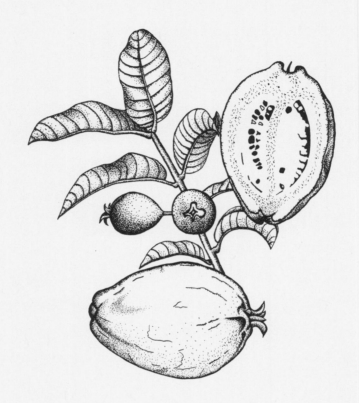

Other names that may be used

Other botanical names: Psidium guienense
Dutch: guajava
French: goyave, goyavier
Indian subcontinent languages: amrut (Hindustani); koiya-pallam (Tamil); pera
    (Singalese)
Portuguese: goiaba
Southeast Asian languages: farang (Thai); jambu batu (Malaysian); vayabas
    (Tagalog)
Spanish: guayaba

Where it grows
Guava is a ubiquitous tree that grows almost everywhere in the tropics and

subtropics on a wide variety of different types of soil. It tolerates both temporary water-logging and high ambient temperatures, but not continuous frost. In some Pacific Islands and in Queensland, Australia, it thrives so well that it has become a major weed of pastures.

Description

The guava is a small tree or large bush, about 6 to 9 m (20 to 30 ft) in height when mature. It has a short trunk and branches freely with a broad, spreading top. The bark is rather distinctive, being greenish-brown to light brown and scaly, peeling off in flakes. The light green leaves are 7 to 18 cm (3 to 7 in) in length, with prominent veins and fine hairs on the underside.

Guava flowers are small, whitish or creamy, and are borne either singly or in small groups on new twigs.

There is a profusion of different types of the fruit, which may be round, ovoid or pear-shaped and weigh from 30 to 450 gm (1 to 16 oz). The outer skin can be very thick or very thin and white, greenish-yellowish, pink or red. The flesh may be white, yellow or pink and contain many or few seeds. Guavas possess a characteristic aroma, ranging from a mild and pleasant musty odour to one that is strong and penetrating. Their flavour can run from very sweet to strongly acid.

Origin and history

The guava is a native of Brazil. It was taken to India by the Portuguese in the seventeenth century and by the Spanish to the Philippines. Gradually the cultivation of this fruit has spread throughout the tropical world.

Notes on cultivation

While guavas will grow on a wide range of soils and in many different climates, they thrive best on neutral soils and where the annual rainfall is 1000 to 1780 mm (40 to 70 in).

It is very easily propagated by seed, that retains viability for approximately 12 months, but improved varieties must be propagated vegetatively — usually by root cuttings. The normal planting distance is 6 to 7½ m (20 to 25 ft). Pruning is desirable as it hastens flowering. Guavas respond to fertilizers and should be fertilized in the same way as citrus.

Young guavas first fruit during the second year of growth. Self-pollination is possible, but cross-pollination is desirable as this results in higher yields. In the subtropics, guavas are seasonal fruiters, but in the tropics they fruit all the year round.

There are many species and varieties and hybrids of different species. *Psidium cattleianum* — the strawberry guava — is particularly valued as a desert fruit.

General uses and recipes

Guavas have five times as high a vitamin C content as orange juice. They are also a fair source of carotene and minerals. The fruit freezes exceptionally well and processes admirably. In some countries the leaves are used as a cure for dysentery, and the wood makes excellent kindling.

GUAVA JUICE

guava pulp (retained from jelly-making, p. 81) cold water

Place the pulp in a preserving pan. Add the water and boil for 15 minutes. Strain the juice. Bottle in sterile containers. Use within 1 week.

ALOHA PUNCH

2 cups white sugar
4 cups cold water
3 cups guava juice
3 cups orange juice
⅓ cup lemon juice

⅓ cup shredded pineapple
grated rind of 1 orange
grated rind of 1 lemon
red food colouring

Put the water and the sugar in a pan. Boil for 3 minutes and cool. Add all the remaining ingredients and stir well. To serve, pour it over cracked ice.

GUAVA PUDDING

8 large, soft, ripe guavas
¼ cup white sugar

1 large, ripe banana
cream and/or grated coconut for
   garnish

Wash the fruit. Peel and cut the guavas into halves. Scoop out the pulp and press it through a coarse sieve to remove the pips. Retain the pulp. Mix the sugar into the pulp. Peel the banana and slice it. Cut up the guava halves and put them into a serving dish with alternate layers of the sliced banana. Pour the pulp over the fruit in the dish. Cover the dish and chill for 2 to 3 hours. Serve with cream and/or grated coconut.

GUAVAS IN SYRUP

ripe guavas
white sugar

water

Wash and dry the guavas. Peel and halve them, and remove the centres. Put the peel and centres in a preserving pan, add a little water and boil them until the peel is soft. Rub it through a fine sieve and measure the volume of the resulting purée. For each cup of purée, allow 1 cup of guava halves, ½ cup of white sugar and a syrup of 1 cup each of water and sugar. Boil the sugar in the water to form the syrup. Put the guava halves in the preserving pan and add sufficient syrup to cover them. Boil until the fruit is half-cooked. Add the purée and sugar, and boil until the fruit is tender. Bottle in sterile jars.

GUAVA CHEESE

ripe guavas   white sugar
lemon juice

Peel the guavas. Press the pulp through a sieve. Weigh. For each 680 g (1½ lb) of pulp, allow 450 g (1 lb) sugar and 1 tablespoon of lemon juice. Add the sugar and lemon juice to the guava pulp in the preserving pan. Bring to the boil, stirring all the time. As soon as the mixture is quite thick and begins to contract from the sides and bottom of the pan it is cooked. Bottle it in sterile jars.

GUAVA SAUCE

570 ml (1 pint) guava juice   100 g + 1 dessertspoon (4 oz) white
3½ dessertspoons cornflour or   sugar
   arrowroot

Blend the cornflour or arrowroot with a little of the guava juice until a smooth paste is formed. Put the remainder of the guava juice in a pan. Add the sugar and bring to the boil. Pour the hot juice over the paste in a separate container, stir the mixture and return it to the pan. Boil for 10 minutes if cornflour is used. If arrowroot is used the mixture should be brought only to the boil and then removed from the heat source. Use hot or cold as a sauce for desserts or for ice cream.

GUAVA JELLY

half-ripe, sour guavas   white sugar
cold water   lemon juice

Wash, top and tail the guavas and place them in a preserving pan. Add sufficient water to cover the fruit and boil gently until it becomes soft and pulpy. Strain the fruit pulp through a jelly bag overnight but do not squeeze it. Measure the volume of the guava liquor. Retain the pulp for Guava Juice (p. 80). For each 6 cups of liquid allow 6 cups of sugar and 1 cup of lemon juice. Add the sugar and the lemon juice to the guava liquor in a preserving pan. Heat gently until the sugar is dissolved. Then boil rapidly until the jelly sets on testing. Store in sterile jars.

GUAVALETS

ripe guavas	¼ teaspoon gelatine
cold water	2 tablespoons cold water
3½ cups white sugar	½ cup chopped nuts

Wash, peel and halve the fruit. Cover the halves with water in a pan and boil until the fruit is tender. Press the fruit through a sieve. Measure the pulp; for each 2 cups of pulp allow 3½ cups of sugar, ¼ teaspoon of gelatine, 2 tablespoons of cold water and ½ cup of chopped nuts. Place the pulp in a pan. Add the sugar and cook over a slow heat, stirring continuously, until the mixture thickens. Put the gelatine and cold water in a basin set over hot water in a saucepan. When the gelatine has dissolved, add the solution to the pulp. Add the nuts and stir them into the pulp. Pour the mixture into a greased shallow tin. Allow it to cool and cut into 2½ cm (1 in) squares. Wrap each piece in waxed paper or cellophane. Store in airtight containers.

GUAVA CATSUP

half-ripe, sour guavas	allspice
cold water	cinnamon
medium onions	ground cloves
vinegar	salt
garlic	preserving sugar
pepper	

Peel the guavas and cut them into quarters. Place these in a preserving pan and add sufficient cold water to cover. Boil until pulpy, then measure the volume. For each 12 cups of guava pulp, allow 5 onions, ¼ cup water, 1½ cups of vinegar, 2 large cloves of garlic, ⅛ teaspoon of pepper, 4 teaspoons of allspice, 3 teaspoons of cinnamon, 2 teaspoons of ground cloves, 1 tablespoon of salt and 6 cups of preserving sugar. Peel and parboil the onions, then cut them up finely and add them to the guava pulp. Add the remaining ingredients to the pulp. Bring to the boil and cook gently for 30 to 40 minutes. Seal the catsup immediately in sterile jars.

16 Jakfruit *Artocarpus integrifolia*

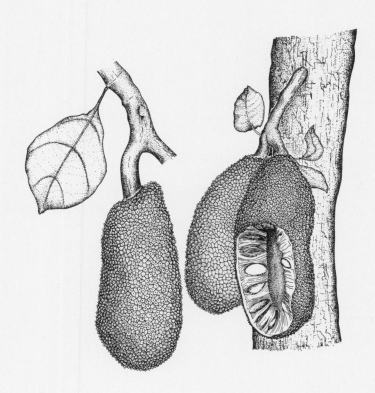

Other names that may be used

Other botanical names: Artocarpus heterophyllus, Artocarpus integra, Artocarpus integrifolius
Dutch: jacca, nagka
Other English: jack, jack-fruit, jaca-tree
French: arbe à pain, jack, jacque, jacquier, pain de singe
Indian subcontinent languages: kos (Singalese); panasa, pilla-kai (Tamil)
Pacific languages: uto ni Idia (Fijian)
Portuguese: jaca, jaca da Bahia
Southeast Asian languages: langka, nangka (Tagalog); jak, nangka (Malaysian); kha-nun (Thai)
Spanish: jaca panapen (Puerto Rico); jacquero (Mexico); pana forestera; pana pepita

Jakfruit

Where it grows
The jakfruit is widely grown throughout tropical lowlands at elevations of less than 1000 m (3300 ft). It is more tolerant of cooler conditions than the breadfruit.

Description
It is a small to medium-sized tree, growing 3 to 7½ m (10 to 25 ft) high, with a straight low-branching trunk which has thick, rough grey bark and a dense crown. The leaves are 10 to 20 cm (4 to 8 in) long and 5 to 10 cm (2 to 4 in) wide, dark green and shiny on the top surface and pale green underneath.

Separate male and female flowers hang on short, thick stems from the trunk and the main branches. The male flowers are small, light-green and numerous, while the female flowers are 4 to 15 cm (1½ to 6 in) long, green, solitary and scented.

Jakfruit is one of the largest edible fruits known and possesses a strong but not particularly unpleasant odour. It is usually more or less oblong, can weigh as much as 32 kg (70 lb), has a thick, hard, spiny skin and a whiteish-yellow to golden-yellow juicy flesh. The seeds are separately embedded in the firm flesh by packed, soft fibres. The individual seed with surrounding flesh is known as a 'bulb'.

Origin and history
Jakfruit is indigenous to the Indian peninsula and was widely cultivated in tropical Asia and on the eastern shore of the African continent before the period of European exploration. It was imported into the American tropics by Europeans.

Notes on cultivation
The tree will grow on almost every soil but prefers deep, well-drained, sandy loams.

It is propagated by seed or vegetatively. The young plant should be shaded and the planting distance is 12 to 15 m (40 to 50 ft). Young trees first fruit when they are seven to eight years old.

Jakfruit flowers and consequently fruits all the year round, the fruits being mature some eight months after flowering.

There are many varieties, ranging from some which produce sweet, juicy aromatic fruit to others whose fruit is acidulous and nearly dry.

General uses and recipes
Jakfruits may be eaten fresh, cooked as a vegetable or preserved in various ways. The rind and the leaves are a useful livestock feed, the seeds can be roasted and taste somewhat like chestnuts, and the yellow heartwood of the tree provides a valuable timber.

CRABS WITH JAKFRUIT

4 medium-sized soft-shelled crabs
unripe jakfruit
½ cup chopped onion
3 medium, sliced tomatoes

1 tablespoon fresh chopped ginger
3 cups coconut cream (page 63)
a dash of monosodium glutamate
a dash of salt

Wash and cut the crabs into halves. Wash the jakfruit and chop into small pieces. Measure out 6 cups of it. Combine all the ingredients in a saucepan with salt to taste. Add the crabs. Cook over medium heat, fairly slowly, until the mixture produces oil. At this stage it is cooked. Serve it hot with rice.

GINATAN

6 jakfruit bulbs
3 tablespoons tapioca
water
1 ripe coconut
1 cup white sugar

4 cooking bananas (plantains)
450 g (1 lb) taro
450 g (1 lb) sweet potatos
450 g (1 lb) yams

Drop the tapioca into boiling water in a saucepan and cook over a medium heat until it is transparent, stirring gently from time to time. Pour off the hot water and immerse the tapioca in cold water. Leave it in the water to cool, then drain. Extract the cream and the first milk from the coconut according to the recipe on page 63. Add the sugar to 2 cups of coconut milk and bring to the boil in a saucepan. Peel the bananas and slice them crossways. Peel and dice the taro, yams and sweet potatoes. Cut the jakfruit bulbs into strips. Add each ingredient to the boiling mixture. Cook on a medium heat, stirring occasionally, until the vegetables are almost cooked. At this stage add the drained, cooked tapioca. When the mixture is completely cooked add one cup of coconut cream. It can be served either hot or cold.

JAKFRUIT CANDY

ripe but firm jakfruit
water

1 tablespoon lime juice
white sugar

Cut the jakfruit and remove the skin. Choose bulbs of about the same size. Cut the end of each bulb and remove the seed. Slice any large bulbs, but leave the small ones whole. Dilute the lime juice in 4½ l (1 gallon) water and soak the jakfruit bulbs in the limewater for 2 hours. Remove the bulbs, wash them thoroughly and blanch them in boiling water for 2 minutes. Then dip them immediately into cold water. Drain. Make a syrup by dissolving 2 parts of white sugar in 1 part of water. Add the bulbs to the syrup and boil for 5 minutes. Leave them in the syrup to soak for 1 week. Each day remove the bulbs, boil the syrup for 2 minutes, then return the bulbs to the hot syrup. After the week, drain the bulbs. Boil the syrup. Add the bulbs to the boiling syrup and stir gently until all water has evaporated. Remove any excess sugar from the bulbs, and when they are dry wrap each bulb in waxed paper or cellophane and store in sealed jars.

JAKFRUIT PRESERVE

ripe jakfruit   white sugar
water

Cut the jakfruit and remove the skin. Choose ripe but firm bulbs that are more or less uniform in size. Cut the end of each bulb to remove the seed. Slice any large bulbs, but leave the small ones whole. For every 450 g (1 lb) of bulbs, allow 2½ cups of white sugar and 5 cups of water. Dissolve the sugar in the water in a saucepan and boil for 5 minutes. Drop the bulbs in the boiling syrup and cook them rapidly until they are clean and tender. Add boiling water, ½ cup at a time, to the syrup to prevent it becoming too thick before the bulbs are cooked and to ensure that there is sufficient syrup to cover the bulbs at all times. Remove the bulbs from the syrup as soon as they are cooked. Boil the syrup further until it thickens. Pack the bulbs in hot sterile jars and pour the thick syrup over them. Seal the jars.

JAKFRUIT-PINEAPPLE MARMALADE

ripe but firm jakfruits   preserving sugar
chopped pineapple   glucose

Cut and skin the jakfruits. Choose bulbs of about the same size, cut the end from each and remove the seed. Finely slice the bulbs. For each cup of sliced bulbs allow 3 cups of chopped pineapple, 2 cups of preserving sugar and ½ cup of glucose. Mix all the ingredients in a preserving pan. Cook until the mixture thickens and the marmalade sets on testing. Seal in sterilized jars.

JAKFRUIT-APPLE MARMALADE

ripe but firm jakfruit   preserving sugar
apple pulp

Cut and skin the jakfruits. Choose bulbs of about the same size, cut the end from each and remove the seed. Finely slice the bulbs. For each 2 cups of sliced bulbs allow 1 cup of apple pulp and 3 cups of preserving sugar. Mix all the ingredients together in a preserving pan. Cook until the mixture thickens and the marmalade sets on testing. Seal it in sterilized jars.

17 Langsat *Lansium domesticum*

Other names that may be used

Dutch: doekoe
French: lansium
Portuguese: árbol de lanze
Southeast Asian languages: langsat, duku (Malaysian); lonsones (Tagalog)
Spanish: árbol de lanze

Where it grows
Langsat is found throughout Southeast Asia and particularly in Malaysia,

Indonesia and the Philippines. It has been introduced to India, South America and elsewhere, but is not widely cultivated outside Southeast Asia.

Description

In Malaya, there are two types of tree. One is known as the langsat and the other as the duku. Both grow moderately tall, 15 to 20 m (50 to 66 ft) high, and have straight trunks. The langsat has slender, upright branches, while the duku is a handsomer tree with a wide crown. The bark of the langsat is pinkish-brown, while that of the duku is brown.

Langsat leaves are large, 30 to 50 cm (12 to 20 in) long, dark green and shiny on the upper surface and light green and dull on the lower; the leaves of the duku are paler.

Flowers are borne on long stalks that hang from the trunk or the larger branches. Flower stalks of the duku are usually shorter than those of the langsat. The flowers are small and yellowish-green or light yellow in colour.

Fruits hang in drooping clusters of closely-packed berries, like grapes on a single stem. They vary in size from 2½ to 5 cm (1 to 2 in) in diameter, and in shape from round to oval. Fruits of the duku are usually rounder and larger than those of the langsat. The ripe fruit of both trees has a thin, tough skin which is pale yellow with brown blemishes. The flesh is usually white, though in some varieties of duku it is pink, translucent, very juicy and sweet or acidic (according to the variety). In the langsat, the skin exudes a milky, sticky juice. The seeds are very bitter.

Origin and history

The langsat and duku originated in the Malay archipelago. It has been suggested that the langsat might be the wild form of the duku and that the seedless variety of the latter may have been evolved during cultivation.

Notes on cultivation

This tree thrives best in an equatorial climate on deep, rich, well-drained, sandy, loam soils. It is slow growing and takes approximately 15 years from planting the seed to fruiting maturity. It may crop twice a year, but the main crop in Malaysia and Indonesia ripens from December through February. If planted in an orchard, it should be spaced at 8 to 10 m (26 to 33 ft) intervals.

General uses and recipes

This is a very popular fresh fruit in Malaysia, Indonesia and the Philippines. Care must be taken when peeling to remove all the astringent skin and, when eating, not to bite the bitter seeds. The stickiness of the latex can be largely removed by dipping the fruit in boiling water to coagulate the latex.

LANGSAT JAM

ripe langsats   preserving sugar

Wash, peel and separate the segments. Remove the seeds and cut the segments into 5 pieces each. To each cup of pulp, allow ¾ cup of preserving sugar. Add the sugar to the pulp in a preserving pan. Bring the mixture to the boil, continue to boil vigorously, with constant stirring, until a setting test shows that the jam is cooked. Seal in sterile jars.

18 Mango *Mangifera indica*

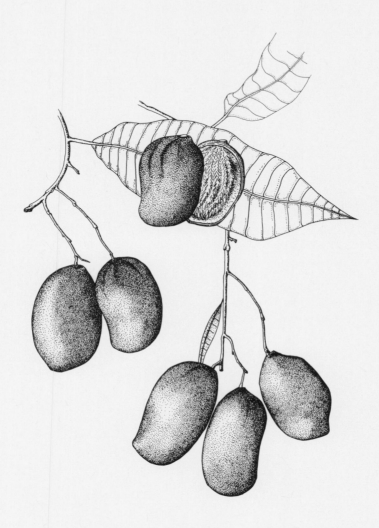

Other names that may be used

Dutch: mangga (Indonesia); manja (Surinam)
East African languages: embe, mwembe (Swahili)
French: arbre de mango, mangier, mango, mangue, manguier
Indian subcontinent languages: amba (Singalese); manga (Tamil)
Portuguese: manga (Brazil); mangiera (Goa); muembo

Mango

Southeast Asian languages: manga (Tagalog); mangga (Malaysian); ma-muang
    (Thai)
Spanish: mango
West African languages: a-mangkoro, a-manko (Temne); mangoro (Yoruba,
    Hausa); mangolo (Ibo); mangro (Creole); mangwaro (Hausa); mangwi
    (Mende); mano, manno (Twi)

Where it grows

Mangoes are found throughout the tropics and in regions of the subtropics where the minimum mean temperature is above 15°C (59°F). The tree grows particularly well in monsoon climates.

Description

It is a medium to large tree growing up to 18 m (60 ft) high when mature, with a more or less straight trunk and brownish-grey bark. The young leaves are reddish-violet or bronze coloured, but when mature they become dark-green and glossy on top and yellowish-green underneath. The leaves then are 10 to 40 cm (4 to 16 in) long and 2½ to 10 cm (1 to 4 in) wide. Mango leaves create a dense foliage that would make an ideal shade tree, were it not for the fact that it is a favourite haunt of mosquitoes.

The flowers are yellowish-green and the fruits are highly variable in shape, weight (170 to 680 gm (6 to 24 oz)) and taste. They are produced in clusters, each fruit hanging from a stalk that sometimes can be very long. The fruit's skin is thick and coloured from yellowish-green to red. The flesh surrounds a large, hard stone and may be light yellow to deep orange, and very tough and fibrous or almost completely free from fibre. The poorest varieties invariably have a turpentine-like taste, but the best varieties have a superlative taste.

Origin and history

Mangoes are indigenous to the Indo-Burmese region of Asia and wild trees are still found in the forests of Assam and the Chittagong hills. They have been cultivated for at least 6000 years and there are now more than 1000 commercial varieties grown in India. Indian stories and legends are full of references to the mango and it must have been used on a vast scale in the past as Akbar, a ruler of northern India in the sixteenth century, is said to have planted an orchard containing 100,000 trees. From India it was spread throughout Southeast and East Asia, being grown in southern China by the seventh century. It was imported into the southern Philippines in the fifteenth century and spread to the northern Philippine islands by the sixteenth century. The Spanish imported it into their American colonies from the Philippines during the eighteenth century. The Portuguese spread the cultivation of it to East and South Africa during the sixteenth and seventeenth centuries and first planted it at Bahia, in Brazil, about 1700.

Notes on cultivation

The mango will thrive on any well-drained soil, but it prefers sandy loams or medium clays. The soils must not be too acid and the roots of this tree will not tolerate water-logging.

It may be propagated from seed or vegetatively, but superior varieties must be propagated vegetatively by budding or grafting. Mangoes are spaced at 10 to 12 m (33 to 39 ft) intervals; they respond to fertilizers and need little pruning. The young plants require shade.

Vegetatively-propagated trees first fruit at four years of age, but seedling trees require six to ten years before they fruit. The yield of trees begins to decline once they are 40 years old.

Mango trees are notoriously irregular in bearing fruit. They flower during the dry season and in the equatorial tropics they may fruit only occasionally, as continuous rainfall reduces the chances of a proper pollination taking place. In tropical regions where a dry season coincides with flowering, they may fruit twice a year, the out-of-season crop being very light and dependent on the rainfall. In the subtropics they may become biennial bearers, producing heavy crops in alternate years.

General uses and recipes

Ripe mangoes contain 10 to 20 per cent sugar and are a useful source of carotene and vitamin C.

The best dessert mangoes are delicious and so juicy that they are difficult to eat with elegance. It is said that the only place in which one can really enjoy eating a dessert mango is in the bath.

Certain varieties are excellent when eaten green; others may be picked when they are very young and pickled like walnuts. Mangoes are widely used in chutneys and hot pickles, and make excellent jams and jellies.

BOTTLED MANGOES

| firm ripe mangoes | water |
| sugar | |

Peel and slice the mangoes; drop the slices in cold water. Drain them. Pack the fruit in sterile jars. Make a syrup with equal parts of sugar and water. Boil and pour the syrup over the fruit in the jars. Half-seal the jars. Place them in a water bath and heat for 20 minutes. Seal the jars completely and allow them to stand upside-down for a short period, until the fruit no longer rises to the top.

MANGO ICE-CREAM

1 large ripe mango	¼ cup white sugar
3 egg yolks	1 egg white
570 ml (1 pint) milk	½ teaspoon of vanilla flavouring

Beat the eggs in a basin. Scald the milk and pour it slowly over the egg yolks, stirring all the time. Mix the sugar and egg white together and add it to the milk and egg yolks. Place the mixture in a basin over a pan of boiling water and cook it for 10 minutes, stirring all the time. Leave it to cool. Wash and peel the mango, cut it into small pieces and add it to the cold custard. Stir the vanilla in well and freeze it in an ice-tray.

MANGO SWEETS

ripe firm mangoes	white sugar

Wash and peel the mangoes. Scrape the flesh out of the fruit with a stainless steel knife or spoon. Measure the volume of the pulp. For each cup of pulp, allow ½ cup of sugar. Place the fruit and the sugar in a preserving pan and boil until the mixture thickens, stirring all the time. Test the texture by dropping a little into a glass of cold water. If the mixture forms into small balls it is ready to turn out on to a sugar-covered board. Roll the mixture into small sausages and allow it to cool. Cut into small pieces and wrap each piece in wax paper or cellophane.

MANGO JAM

ripe mangoes	preserving sugar

Peel the fruit, scrape away the ripe flesh, using a stainless steel knife or fork, and measure the volume of pulp. For each cupful, allow ½ cup of preserving sugar. Place the pulp and sugar in a preserving pan. Boil, stirring all the time, until the mixture thickens. When the jam sets on testing, bottle it in hot sterile jars. Seal.

MANGO JELLY

green mangoes and water	white sugar
lemon juice	

Wash and stone the mangoes; cut them into small pieces. Place stones and fruit in a preserving pan, cover with water and boil until pulpy. Strain the mixture slowly through a jelly bag. Measure the volume of the liquor. For each cup of liquid, allow 1¼ cups of sugar and 1 teaspoon of lemon juice. Place all together in a preserving pan and boil until the jelly sets. Store in sterile jars.

PICKLED MANGOES

1¾ kg (4 lb) approximately very young green mangoes picked before the stone has formed
510 g (18 oz) salt
6¾ l (12 pints) water

85 g (3 oz) fresh ginger
85 g (3 oz) cloves
55 g (2 oz) mustard seed
a little mace
2¼ l (4 pints) vinegar

Make a brine by dissolving 170 g (6 oz) of the salt in 2¼ l (4 pints) of the water in a bowl. Place the mangoes in the brine and soak them for 3 days. Pour off the brine and put the mangoes in a new brine of 170 g (6 oz) of salt and 2¼ l (4 pints) of water. Leave them in it for a further 3 days, then repeat the process once more, using the remaining salt and water. Strain the fruit on the tenth day. Put the vinegar in a preserving pan; bruise the ginger and add it to the vinegar. Tie the spices in a muslin bag. Add the spice bag and boil the vinegar for 10 minutes. Pack the mangoes in hot sterile jars. Pour the hot vinegar mixture over the fruit and seal the jars.

MANGO CHUTNEY

2¾ kg (6 lb) green unripe mangoes
1¾ l (3 pints) vinegar
1¾ kg (4 lb) sugar
55 g (2 oz) fresh ginger
85 g (3 oz) onions

55 g (2 oz) garlic
140 g (5 oz) salt
30 g (1 oz) chillies
450 g (1 lb) raisins or sultanas

Wash the mangoes, remove the stones and cut the flesh into small pieces. Place the vinegar in a preserving pan, dissolve the sugar in the vinegar and boil the mixture for 30 minutes. Add the mangoes to the vinegar solution. Scrape and wash the ginger, cut into small pieces. Peel the onions and cut them into small slices. Peel and crush the garlic. Add these, with the remaining ingredients, to the vinegar solution. Boil until the fruit is soft. Place in hot, sterile jars and seal.

19 Mangosteen *Garcinia mangostana*

Other names that may be used

Dutch: manggis, manggistan
French: mangoustan, mangoustanier, mangouste, mangoustier
Indian subcontinent languages: mangus (Singalese); manguskai, mangustai
    (Tamil); mangusta; mangustan
Portuguese: mangostão
Southeast Asian languages: manggis (Tagalog); manggis; manggista (Indonesian);
    manggis, mesta, sementah (Malaysian); mung-khut (Thai)
Spanish: mangostán

Where it grows
The mangosteen tree is found only in regions having a hot, humid, equatorial
climate and is common only in Southeast Asia.

Description
The tree is a slow-growing evergreen of medium size that attains a maximum
height of approximately 14 m (45 ft). The leaves are short-stalked, leathery

and dark green. The flowers are of a yellowish hue tinged with red and are borne at the end of the twigs.

Mangosteen fruits are handsome. They are like large berries, round but slightly flattened at both ends, with a smooth, rich-looking, red-purple thick rind, partially covered with the flower petals that remain attached as the fruit ripens. Inside the rind the pulp is divided into five to seven segments, some containing a seed. The flesh within the segments is whitish and juicy, and possesses a delicious, delicate flavour.

Origin and history

Little is known as to the history of cultivation of the mangosteen. In fact the fruit is almost unknown outside Southeast Asia.

Notes on cultivation

This fruit is undoubtedly difficult to propagate, and this may be one reason why it is seldom found outside Southeast Asia. Seeds do not germinate very well, have a low viability and must be planted a few days after being removed from the fruit. Vegetative propagation is practised, but it is not easy.

Mangosteens appear to grow in almost any soil within the equatorial tropics. Seedlings should be transferred when they are about two years old and planted 7½ m (25 ft) apart. The tree matures very slowly so that its age at first fruiting can be anywhere between eight and 15 years.

Fruiting is irregular and the season is short. The fruit should not be harvested until they are mature. A fully-mature tree can produce up to 500 fruit per year.

General uses and recipes

The fruit is eaten fresh or used to make preserves. In order to eat the fresh fruit, the initiated may break the berry by hand. The uninitiated are advised to make a circular cut with a sharp knife. The upper portion of the rind is then removed, to reveal the white segments sitting loosely in the lower portion of the rind. These segments are fresh and juicy and possess an extreme delicacy of flavour and many people believe that the mangosteen is the most superb of all tropical fruits.

MANGOSTEEN PRESERVE

ripe mangosteens   sugar
water

Make a circular cut in the skin of the fruit with a sharp knife and scoop out the white fleshy segments. Make a thin syrup by heating 1 part of sugar in 3 parts of water until the sugar dissolves. Drop the segments immediately into the syrup to prevent discolouration. Now make a thick syrup by dissolving 1 part of sugar in 1 part of water. Pack the segments in sterile jars and pour in the thick syrup. Partially-seal the jars. Sterilize them by standing them in a boiling water bath for 25 minutes. Seal completely.

MANGOSTEEN JAM (1)

ripe mangosteens   preserving sugar

Make a circular cut in the mangosteens with a sharp knife and scoop out the fleshy white segments. Measure their volume. For each cup of mangosteen segments allow ¾ cup of sugar. Place in a preserving pan and bring to the boil. Cook rapidly, stirring constantly until the jam is ready. Test the setting quality. When ready, remove the jam from the heat but continue stirring for 5 minutes in order to distribute the fruit evenly in the jellied mass. Seal in sterilized jars.

MANGOSTEEN JAM (2)

12 ripe mangosteens   preserving sugar
cloves

Make a circular hole in the mangosteen with a sharp knife, scoop out the fleshy white segments and weigh them. To each 450 g (1 lb) of fruit, add an equal weight of sugar and 3 cloves. Place all in a preserving pan. Boil together for 15 to 20 minutes. Test for setting. When the jam is ready remove the cloves. Seal in sterilized jars.

20 *Otaheite-Apple* *Spondias cytherea*

Other names that may be used

Other botanical names: Spondias dulcis
Dutch: fransimopé (Surinam)
Other English: ambarella, golden apple, Tahitian quince, great hog plum
French: prunier d'Amerique
Pacific languages: wi (Fijian)
Portuguese: cajá-manga (Brazil)
Southeast Asian languages: hevi (Tagalog); kedongdong, kedongdong manis
    (Malaysian); ma-kok-farang (Thai); ledondorg (Indonesian)
Spanish: ciruelo calentano, ciruelo dulce (Cuba; ciruelo de husso (Venezuela);
    ciruelo jobo (Colombia); hobo colorado; jobo

Otaheite-Apple

Where it grows

The otaheite-apple thrives in lowland, humid tropics up to a height of 700 m (2300 ft), particularly in Southeast Asia, the Pacific Islands, the Caribbean and South America. It can also be grown in the warmer regions of the subtropics such as Florida.

Description

It is a medium to tall tree with a straight trunk, often attaining a height of 18 m (60 ft), the bark being whitish to greyish-brown. The leaves are hairless, dark green above and pale green below, and crowded at the end of small branches. They give off a strong resinous smell when bruised.

The flowers are small and are usually yellowish-white. Fruits are thin-skinned and amber when ripe, being somewhat similar in shape to the mango. They consist of a somewhat acid, scanty, white or pale yellow pulp surrounding a rather large, thin, fibrous stone with a slightly resinous but not unpleasant odour.

Origin and history

This tree is probably indigenous to the Pacific Islands and has been introduced into Southeast Asia. It has since been cultivated in the Caribbean and South America.

Notes on cultivation

It appears to thrive in almost any type of soil and is usually grown from seed, but superior types may be propagated by cuttings or by budding. Young trees are planted at 12 to 14 m (40 to 46 ft) intervals and require shade during their first year. They fruit for the first time at about four years from planting and in the humid tropics yield throughout the year.

General uses and recipes

Otaheite-apple is usually too sour to be eaten fresh, but it makes excellent preserves and jams and can also be used as an ingredient of stews and curries.

OTAHEITE-APPLE JELLY

ripe otaheite-apples   preserving sugar
water   lemon juice

Wash the otaheite-apples, cut them into small pieces and place in a preserving pan. Cover the fruit with water and boil until soft. Strain the pulp through a muslin bag hung above the pan and allow it to drip overnight. Measure the volume of juice. Add 1 cup of sugar and ½ teaspoon of lemon juice to each cup of the otaheite-apple juice and boil until the mixture jellies. Store in sterile jars.

OTAHEITE-APPLE CHUTNEY

2¾ kg (6 lb) ripe otaheite-apples
225 g (½ lb) each sultanas and raisins
2 cloves of garlic
1 dozen cloves
1 whole nutmeg

1½ kg (3 lb) preserving sugar
4 chillies (optional)
25 g (1 oz) salt
1.1 l (2 pints) vinegar

Wash, slice and place the fruit in a preserving pan with the sultanas and raisins. Peel and crush the garlic and add it to the pan with the cloves. Grate the nutmeg into the pan. Add the sugar, chillies, salt and vinegar, and slowly boil together for 2 hours. Store in sterile jars.

21 Papaya *Carica papaya*

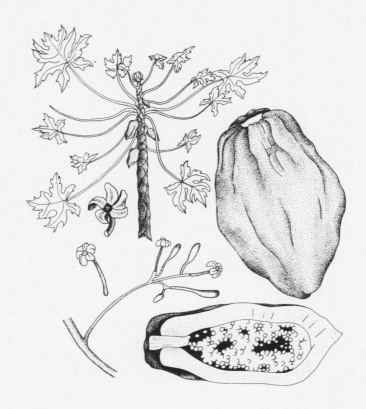

Other names that may be used

Other botanical names: Papaya carica
Dutch: meloenboom, papaja
Other English: melon tree, mummy apple, pawpaw
French: figuier des îles, papaye, papayer
Indian subcontinent languages: pappali (Tamil); pepol (Singalese)
Pacific languages: maoli, oleti (Fijian)
Portuguese: mamão
Spanish: fruta bomba (Cuba); papaya (Colombia); melon zapote (Mexico)
Southeast Asian languages: betek, kepaya, ketela (Malaysian); ma-la-koh (Thai)
  pepaya (Indonesian)
West African languages: adiba, aduba (Ewe); am-papai (Temne); borefere, brofre
  (Twi); budi-lede (Fula); fakai, fakali (Mende); gbegbere, ibepe (Yoruba);
  gwanda, gwadda (Hausa); go (Krobo); ogede, ojo, oyibo (Ibo); popo (Creole)

Where it grows
Papaya plants grow everywhere in the tropics and warmer subtropics below an altitude of 1000 m (3300 ft).

Description
The papaya is a giant herbaceous plant rather than a tree. It is very fast growing, attains a height of 2 to 10 m (6½ to 33 ft), is short-lived and normally possesses an unbranched grey or greyish-brown trunk, 10 to 30 cm (4 to 12 in) in diameter, topped with an umbrella of large handsome dark or yellow-green leaves. If the single trunk is damaged it will branch during regrowth.

The male and female flowers are usually borne on separate trunks, but some trees are bisexual. The male flowers are on drooping, many-flowered stalks, 25 to 100 cm (10 to 39 in) in length. They flower before the female trees and are fragrant. The female flowers appear singly, close to the trunk. It is normal to leave one male tree for every 15 to 50 female trees in a papaya orchard.

Papaya fruits are very varied in shape, size and flavour. They may be almost round, pear-shaped or cylindrical and may weigh from ½ to 9 kg (1 to 20 lb). The skin of most varieties turns yellow or orange when the fruit is ripe, but some are green and others are speckled with yellow. The ripe flesh, which may be pale yellow, orange or red, surrounds a central cavity in which there is a mass of small black seeds. Female plants usually produce superior-quality fruit to those gathered from bisexual plants.

Origin and history
The papaya is indigenous to the American tropics and was first discovered by the Spanish explorers in Panama. The cultivation of this fruit had already spread into the coastal districts of tropical Africa and Asia by the end of the sixteenth century.

Notes on cultivation
Papayas need light, well-drained soils rich in humus. They are gross feeders and require adequate quantities of fertilizer, preferably compost and/or animal manure together with chemical fertilizers.

Papayas are grown from seed, which should be selected from fruit of good flavour obtained from productive trees. Several seeds are planted and the seedlings thinned. A final thinning should be made as soon as the sex of the trees can be determined. Spacing should be 2 to 3 m (6½ to 10 ft), depending on the size of the variety, and the young seedlings should be sheltered. Papaya trees mature in 12 to 18 months and possess a life span of three to ten years. One of the best of the dessert varieties is the small 'solo' papaya.

General uses and recipes

The ripe fruit contains little starch but 7 to 9 per cent of sugar. They are used for dessert and are most delicious when chilled and served with lemon juice. The fruit bruises easily and are choicest when eaten as soon as possible after picking. Ripe fruit can also be used in the preparation of cold drinks, ice-cream and sherbet.

Unripe papayas can be used as a vegetable or for pickles and chutneys.

The stems and leaves of papaya contain small amounts of the alkaloid, carpain, which is used as a heart stimulant. The plant also produces the enzyme, papain, used as a meat tenderizer. Papain is produced on a commercial scale by lancing the surface of immature fruit, collecting the latex that is exuded and drying it to form a white powder. In the home, meat may be wrapped in papaya leaves before cooking to make it tender.

STUFFED PAPAYA

1 large, firm, ripe papaya
450 g (1 lb) minced meat (½ pork
    and ½ beef is most suitable)
1 large onion
1 egg

salt and pepper
fat
1 cup crisp breadcrumbs
tomato sauce or gravy

Wash and peel the papaya. Cut a small square opening at the stem end of the fruit and remove the seeds. Retain the square of flesh. Place the minced meat in a bowl. Peel and chop the onion, and add it to the meat. Add the egg and seasoning to taste. Mix well. Stuff the papaya with the meat mixture and replace the square of flesh. Place the papaya on a greased baking dish, dot it with a little fat and bake for 1 hour at 180°C (350°F), Gas Mark 4. Sprinkle the breadcrumbs over the papaya before serving with tomato sauce or a good gravy.

PAPAYA DELIGHT

almost ripe papayas
115 g (4 oz) brown sugar
½ teaspoon ground ginger
½ teaspoon lemon juice
280 g (10 oz) shortcrust pastry

85 g (3 oz) raisins or sultanas
1 fresh coconut, grated
milk
white sugar

Wash, peel, and seed the papayas; cut up into small pieces. Weigh out 450 g (1 lb). Put the fruit in a preserving pan with the brown sugar, ginger and lemon juice. Boil until tender. Leave to cool. Line a medium-sized pie-dish with one third of the pastry. Add the raisins or sultanas to the papaya mixture, and pour half the mixture into the pie-dish. Sprinkle half the coconut over the papaya mixture. Place half of the remaining pastry over the papaya and coconut. Repeat the process using the remainder of the papaya, the other half of the coconut and the last of the pastry. Brush milk over the pastry and sprinkle white sugar over the top of the pie. Bake in an oven at 230°C (450°F), Gas Mark 8, until pastry is baked. Serve hot or cold.

PAPAYA SHERBET

ripe papayas
3 tablespoons lemon juice
1 cup white sugar

juice of ½ an orange
1½ cups milk

Wash, halve, seed and sieve the papayas to produce a pulp. Measure out 1½ cups of pulp. Mix the fruit pulp, orange juice and lemon juice in a pan. Warm the milk; dissolve the sugar in it. Gradually stir the sweetened milk into the papaya mixture. Freeze, stirring at half-hour intervals.

PAPAYA ICE-CREAM

ripe papayas
juice of ½ an orange
3 tablespoons lemon juice

1 cup evaporated milk or fresh cream
1 cup white sugar

Wash, halve, seed and sieve the papayas. Measure out 1½ cups of the pulp. Mix the pulp with the fruit juices in a pan. Warm the evaporated milk or cream and dissolve the sugar in it. Stir the sweetened evaporated milk or cream into the papaya mix. Freeze, stirring at half-hour intervals.

PAPAYA CHUTNEY

2¼ kg (5 lb) green papayas
225 g (½ lb) onions
1 kg (2 lb) sugar
340 g (12 oz) raisins or sultanas
55 g (2 oz) ground ginger

1 tablespoon curry powder
¼ tablespoon salt
¼ tablespoon cayenne pepper
1.1 l (2 pints) vinegar

Wash, peel and cut the papayas into 2½ cm (1 in) cubes. Peel and slice the onions. Place all the ingredients in a preserving pan and boil gently for 3 hours. Bottle in sterile jars.

PAPAYA PICKLES (1), (2) and (3)

green, white-fleshed but fully grown   salt
   papayas   garlic
20 small onions   fresh ginger root
red and green sweet peppers   vinegar

Wash, peel and shred or grate the papayas. Measure the volume. For each 8 cups of papaya, use the following quantities: 1 cup salt, 1 head of garlic, 20 small onions, 2 each red and green peppers and ½ cup peeled and chopped ginger root. Mix the salt into the papaya, working it well with the hand. Strain through a cheese cloth, squeezing out all the water. Use sufficient vinegar to cover the papayas, and soak them overnight. The following day drain off the vinegar. Peel and chop the garlic, onions and ginger root, and wash, seed and chop the sweet peppers. Add all these ingredients to the papaya. Mix. Pack the mixture loosely into sterile jars. Now use one of the three sugar-vinegar-salt mixtures according to the type of pickle desired. The following quantities are suitable for 8 cups of shredded papaya.

SOUR PICKLE (1)

1 cup vinegar   ½ cup preserving sugar
1 teaspoon salt

SWEET AND SOUR PICKLE (2)

1 cup vinegar   ⅔ cup preserving sugar
1 teaspoon salt

SWEET PICKLE (3)

1 cup vinegar   ¾ cup preserving sugar
1 teaspoon salt

Dissolve the sugar and salt by heating in the vinegar. Then cool and pour it over the papaya packed in the jars. Remove air bubbles from the jars by inserting a fork and wiggling it in the mixture. Seal the jars. These pickles will keep for only 2 to 3 weeks.

PAPAYA PICKLE (4)

half-ripe papayas
vinegar
cloves
bay leaves

cold water
preserving sugar
red peppers

Wash and peel the papayas, slice them into finger lengths and measure the volume. For every 8 cups of fruit use 2 cups each of cold water and vinegar, 4 cups of preserving sugar, 12 cloves, 5 red peppers (chopped) and 4 bay leaves. Place the papayas and water in a preserving pan and boil for 5 minutes. Drain. Add the remaining ingredients to the papaya. Boil together for 15 minutes. Seal in sterile jars.

22 Passion Fruit

The genus *Passiflora* includes several hundred species of plants, the majority being indigenous to the American tropics. Three species are widely cultivated for their fruit: *Passiflora edulis,* the purple-shelled passion fruit; *Passiflora laurifolia,* the yellow-shelled passion fruit; and *Passiflora quadrangularis,* the granadilla. Details of and recipes for the last have already been described on pages 75-77.

As the purple and yellow passion fruits are cultivated and utilized in more or less the same manner, they are described together in this section. The major difference between them is that the purple-shelled passion fruit is hardier and can be grown in warm, temperate and Mediterranean climates, whereas the yellow-shelled passion fruit thrives only in tropical or subtropical climates.

PURPLE-SHELLED PASSION FRUIT   *Passiflora edulis*

Other names that may be used

Dutch: eiervrucht; kappoeweri-markoessa (Surinam); passievrucht
Other English: granadilla fruit, purple-fruited granadilla, purple granadilla, purple grenadilla, simitoo, sweet cup (Ceylon)

108

French: grenadella, grenadellina, grenadille, marie tambour, pomme liane
Portuguese: maracujá, maracujá peroba, maracujá redondo
Southeast Asian languages: linmangkon (Thai)
Spanish: granadilla; parcha (Venezuela)

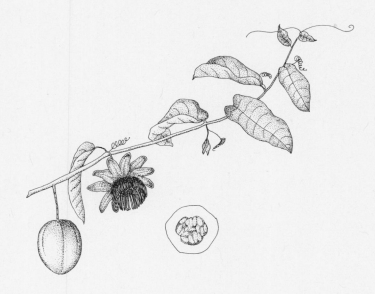

YELLOW-SHELLED PASSION FRUIT   *Passiflora laurifolia*

Other names that may be used

Dutch: makoesar
Other English: bell apple; Jamaica honeysuckle; pomme d'Or; water-lemon;
    yellow granadilla (West Indies)
French: pomme-liane, pomme de liane
Portuguese: maracujá commun
Southeast Asian languages: buah susu (Malaysian); sa-wa-rot (Thai)

Where it grows
Purple-shelled passion fruit is widely grown in subtropical and upland tropical
regions above 1000 m (3300 ft). It is also grown in some warm temperate
countries, such as New Zealand, and in Mediterranean climatic regions. The
yellow-shelled passion fruit is grown only in the lowland tropics and thrives
particularly well in oceanic tropical islands.

Description
The purple-shelled passion fruit is a perennial vine, with light or dark green,
creeping stems capable of growing 25 to 80 m (82 to 262 ft) long and closely-

109

coiled tendrils that may be 20 to 40 cm (8 to 16 in) in total length. The leaves are three-lobed, 10 to 18 cm (4 to 7 in) long and 12 to 20 cm (5 to 8 in) broad, shiny dark green on the surface and light green underneath.

The flowers are borne singly and are whitish or pale violet; the fruits are round or ovoid, about the size of a hen's egg. The thick skin is brownish-violet but on ripening it quickly wrinkles, giving the fruit a wizened appearance. The sweet-sour fruit pulp is inseparable from the dark-violet or black seeds.

Yellow-shelled passion fruit vines are very similar, but the leaves are different, being thick and oblong in shape. The flower is white with red spots and the fruit is much larger and usually round. When it is ripe, it is light yellow or yellow spotted with white. The shell is much harder and thicker than the purple-shelled passion fruit and the pulp is white or yellowish-white, very juicy and slightly acid.

Origin and history
The purple-shelled passion fruit is native to southern Brazil and was not widely distributed throughout the subtropics until the end of the nineteenth century. The yellow-shelled passion fruit is indigenous to the West Indies and the north-eastern region of tropical South America. It still has a restricted distribution but is gradually being introduced into the tropical lowland regions of Africa and Asia.

Notes on cultivation
The purple-shelled passion fruit will thrive on almost any soil as long as climatic conditions are suitable. It is propagated by seeds, layering or from cuttings taken from the mature wood. Seeds germinate in two to four weeks and the seedlings or young vegetative material are very tender and should be protected. The vines should be supported on wires or trellises at least 2 to 3 m (6½ to 10 ft) high and planted 5 m (16 ft) apart.

The age at first fruiting is approximately one year, and the maximum life of a vine about five to six years. Fruit is produced only on the new growth and the fruits should be allowed to drop to ensure that they are ripe. The flowers open at dawn and close at noon, and pollination by hand can be of assistance in ensuring good crops.

The culture of the yellow-shelled passion fruit is approximately the same as that of the purple-shelled type. One difference is that the flowers open at noon and close at sunset and hand-pollination is almost essential to ensure a good crop.

General uses and recipes
The pulp of both types of passion fruit can be used as a dessert or to make cold drinks, fruit salads, sherbets and jellies. Pulp used for desserts is always improved by chilling and is obtained by halving the fruit lengthways and scooping it out with a spoon.

PASSION FRUITADE

ripe passion fruit   water
sugar

Cut the fruits into halves. Scoop out the pulp with a spoon. Add water and whisk briskly or blend. (You will need ½ cup water to 2 cups of pulp.) Strain the mixture through a sieve to remove the seeds. Measure the volume of juice. To each cup of juice use ½ cup sugar. Dissolve the sugar in the juice and store the fruitade in sterile bottles. Serve, diluted according to taste, with ice.

PASSION FRUIT JELLY

ripe passion fruit   gelatine
sugar

Halve the fruit, scoop out the pulp, add water and whisk it or put it through the blender. Measure the juice. For each cup of juice use 1 tablespoon of gelatine and ½ cup of sugar. Dissolve the gelatine in a small volume of the heated juice. Add the rest of the juice and mix. Stir in the sugar. Set in a bowl or baked pie-crust shell.

23 *Pineapple* *Ananas comosus*

Other names that may be used

Other botanical names: Bromelia ananas, Bromelia comosa, Ananassa sativa,
    Ananus sativus
Dutch: ananas
French: ananas, pain de sucre
Indian subcontinent languages: annasi (Singalese)
Pacific languages: vadra (Fijian)
Portuguese: abacaxi, ananas (Brazil); ananas de Caraguatá
Southeast Asian languages: ma-kha-nat, sappa-rot (Thai); nanas (Malaysian)
Spanish: piña
West African languages: abarba (Hausa); abrobe (Twi); ablendi, atoto (Ewe);
    akwolu, akwu-olu (Ibo); a-nanas (Temne); blefota (Krobo); mbelu, nesi
    (Mende); nanas (Fula); opeyinbo (Yoruba); painapul (Creole)

Where it grows

Pineapples can be grown throughout the lowland areas of the tropics, in upland areas up to 920 m (3000 ft) near the equator and in some of the warmer regions of the subtropics where the annual mean temperature is above 21°C (70°F). They were widely cultivated in greenhouses in Europe during the eighteenth century.

Description

The pineapple is a small, herbaceous perennial with long, 60 to 120 cm (23½ to 47 in), stiff, grass-like leaves arranged in a spiral around a short stem. The leaves may or may not be spiny along the edges. There is one active growing point, located at the stem apex, that eventually becomes a flower. This is well adapted to catch and hold dew and rain.

The fruit develops from the flower at the end of the stem and consists of a hundred or more small, seedless fruits fused together. It is oval or cylindrical in shape, varies in weight from ½ to 5 kg (1 to 10 lb) and has a rough, scaly rind that may be greenish, yellowish or orange. All varieties of pineapple are self-fertile.

Origin and history

Pineapples were originally indigenous to the dry upland areas of the Matto Grosso region of Brazil where at least three wild species are still to be found. Apparently the indigenous Indian peoples spread the cultivation of pineapples widely over Brazil, northeast South America and the West Indies before the fifteenth century.

The first Europeans to see the fruit were in Columbus's second expedition. They found them on the island of Guadeloupe in 1493. The word *anana* for the pineapple has been taken from the Guerani Indian language, and it is these people who may have been partially instrumental in spreading pineapple cultivation widely prior to European exploration of the Americas. The Spanish word *piña* was coined because the fruit bears some resemblance to a pine cone.

The Spanish and the Portuguese soon spread pineapple cultivation throughout the tropical world, as the resistance of the vegetative parts of the plant to desiccation enabled it to remain alive for many months during long sea voyages. It is known, for example, that by 1548 it was being grown in India.

Notes on cultivation

Pineapples thrive best on mildly-acid, sandy loams of medium fertility. The plant will tolerate drought, but adequate soil moisture is necessary for good fruit production.

It is propagated vegetatively from slips, suckers or the crown of the fruit.

113

Commercially, suckers are normally used and are planted at the rate of 37,000 to 50,000 plants per hectare (15,000 to 20,000 per acre) in such a manner that all field operations can be mechanised. Usually they are planted in beds, each consisting of two to five rows, with 46 to 72 cm (18 to 30 in) between the rows and 25 to 46 cm (10 to 18 in) between the beds.

The fruit attains maturity some 12 to 18 months after planting, and replanting is undertaken every two to three years. Fruit ripens almost continuously and should be ripened on the plant if to be of high quality.

Major varieties are: Red Spanish, a medium-sized variety with a pale yellow flesh and a pleasant aroma; Smooth Cayenne, a large canning type; Natal Queen, an excellent small dessert variety with yellow flesh, a crisp texture and a delicate flavour; and Pernambuco, a medium-sized, pale yellow to white-fleshed dessert fruit.

General uses and recipes

Pineapples have a useful content of carotene and vitamin C, and just before they ripen all their starch is transformed into sugar.

The fruit can be used as a fresh dessert fruit, for canning or for the manu-facture of jam and preserves. Where pineapples are processed for canning, the by-products can be used as a fresh or ensiled feed for cattle or can be dehydrated to produce pineapple bran, also used as a livestock feed.

A fine textile known as piña cloth is made in the Philippines from fibres obtained from the leaves.

PINEAPPLE UPSIDE DOWN CAKE

3 cups ripe pineapple chunks	½ cup butter or margarine
2 cups brown sugar	2 cups plain flour
2 teaspoons baking powder	1 egg
1 teaspoon nutmeg	1 teaspoon cinnamon
	½ cup milk

Peel and core sufficient ripe pineapple to give 3 cups and cut the flesh in chunks. Melt the butter in a cake tin, sprinkle 1 cup of sugar into the fat and pour into a mixing bowl. Arrange the pineapple chunks in a pattern in the bottom of the cake tin. Sieve together the flour, baking powder, nutmeg and cinnamon and place them in the mixing bowl. Beat the eggs and 1 cup of sugar together and lightly mix into the flour mixture. Then add the milk and combine. Pour the batter over the fruit in the cake tin and bake for 40-50 minutes at 180°C (350°F), Gas Mark 4. When the cake is baked, turn it out on to a plate and decorate with cherries and nuts. Serve hot or cold.

PINEAPPLE FILLING

1 ripe pineapple
2 teaspoons cornflour
1½ tablespoons lemon juice

½ cup white sugar
2 ripe bananas

Peel and core the pineapple. Grate the fruit and measure ¾ cup of it. Combine the sugar and the cornflour with the fruit in a pan and cook until the mixture thickens. Allow it to cool. Peel and mash the bananas and add them to the pineapple. Stir in the lemon juice. Use this as a filling for cakes, flans, pancakes or sandwiches.

PINEAPPLE JAM

ripe pineapples
preserving sugar

lemon
water

Peel and core the pineapples. Grate the fruit and measure it. For each cup of pineapple, allow 1 lemon, 2 cups of sugar and 1 cup of water. Grate the rind and squeeze the lemon into the pineapple pulp. Place the sugar in a preserving pan, add the water and boil it rapidly to form a thick syrup. Add the pineapple pulp and boil rapidly for 15 minutes. Skim off the scum continuously. Test for setting. When the jam is cooked, store it in sterile jars.

PINEAPPLE HONEY

ripe pinapples
lemon juice

preserving sugar

Peel and core the pineapples. Grate the fruit and measure the volume. For each 8 cups of grated pineapple, use 16 cups of sugar and ¼ cup of lemon juice. Place in a preserving pan and stir until the sugar has dissolved. Leave the mixture to stand for 8 hours, then cook it over a low heat, simmering, until the mixture is transparent and thick. Store in sterile jars.

PINEAPPLE CHUTNEY

1 medium pineapple
2 cups seedless raisins
2 tablespoons ginger
3 cloves of garlic
1½ cups vinegar

3 cups brown sugar
1 tablespoon salt
1 medium onion
3 red peppers
½ cup chopped nuts

Peel and core the pineapple. Cut the flesh into small pieces and put them in a preserving pan. Add the sugar, raisins, salt and ginger to the fruit. Peel and slice the onion, peel and crush the garlic, seed and chop the peppers and add all to the pan. Pour the vinegar over the fruit mixture and simmer until tender. Add the nuts and continue to simmer until the mixture thickens. Store in sterile jars.

CANDIED PINEAPPLE

1 ripe, firm pineapple
1 tablespoon salt
castor sugar

water
white sugar

Peel the pineapple and remove the eyes by cutting spirally down the fruit. Slice the fruit into even rounds and core them. Place the rounds in a preserving pan. Pour 4 cups of water over the pineapple. Add the salt and cook gently for 5 minutes. Drain. Make a syrup by heating 3½ cups of sugar in 4 cups of water. When the sugar has dissolved, pour the syrup over the pineapple in the preserving pan. Boil for 3 to 4 minutes. Make certain that the fruit is covered with syrup. If necessary weigh the fruit down with a plate. Leave for 24 hours. Drain. Save the syrup. Add 55 g (2 oz) of sugar to the syrup. Bring it to the boil and allow to cool. Immerse the fruit in the syrup. Boil for 3 or 4 minutes and leave it to stand for 24 hours. Drain. Save the syrup. Add a further 55 g (2 oz) of sugar to the syrup, again immerse the fruit in it for 3 to 4 minutes and let it stand for 24 hours. Drain, saving the syrup. Repeat as in previous stage but leave the fruit to stand in the syrup for 36 hours. Do this twice. Now add 85 g (3 oz) of sugar to the syrup, put in the fruit and boil it 3 to 4 minutes, but leave the fruit to stand in the syrup for 48 hours. Do this twice, but add 115 g (4 oz) of sugar the second time. Repeat the previous stage, but leave the fruit to stand in the syrup for 72 hours. Drain the fruit, placing it in a wire basket. Save the syrup. Immerse the fruit in a pan of simmering water for 3 seconds. Allow the fruit to dry. Roll the fruit in the castor sugar to complete drying. If a glaze finish is wanted, dissolve ½ cup of sugar in 1 cup of hot water to make a new syrup. Dip each piece of pineapple in this syrup. Dry them in a warm oven, turning them several times. Wrap each piece of fruit in waxed paper or cellophane. Store in air-tight jars. The fruit will keep for up to 3 months.

24 Rambutan *Nephelium lappaceum*

Other names that may be used

Dutch: rambootan
French: letchi chevelu, litchi chevulu, ramboutan, ramboitan
Indian subcontinent languages: ramtum (Singalese)
Southeast Asian languages: ngo, phruan (Thai); rambutan gading (Malaysian); usan (Tagalog)
Spanish: ramustan

Where it grows
Rambutan thrives in the equatorial lowlands, below an altitude of 300 m (984 ft) where the annual rainfall totals at least 2,500 mm (98 in) and is evenly distributed throughout the year. It is not widely cultivated outside Southeast Asia.

Description
Rambutans are ornamental, whether in foliage, flower or fruit. The tree is of medium size, growing on average about 18 m (60 ft) tall, with a straight, high-branched, dark-brownish, barked trunk, and with 5 to 20 cm (2 to 8 in) long

leaves, distinctly veined, dark green on the upper side and yellowish-green below.

The flowers are borne on many-branched flowering stems, 15 to 20 cm (6 to 8 in) long, that grow out from near the end of the twigs. Individual flowers are very small, yellowish-green and with a faint but pleasant scent. There are usually only male or female flowers on one tree.

Round, oblong or ovoid fruit, each about the size of a medium plum, develop in clusters of the most striking appearance. The fruit, green at first, ripens to bright red or orange and is covered with distinctive thick, curved, soft spines. The rind of the fruit is quite thin and tough, and is not attached to the flesh, which is white, translucent and juicy, and is firmly attached to a light brown single seed. The flesh has a pleasing, refreshing, slightly acid taste.

Origin and history
Rambutans originate from the Malaysian peninsula, where wild species are still found in the forests.

Notes on cultivation
This tree thrives best on clay loams with a high content of organic matter. If the rainfall is at all seasonal, irrigation during the dry season may be necessary.

Although the tree can be grown from seed, it is better to plant vegetatively-propagated trees, as some seedling trees will be males and will not fruit. Vegetative propagation can be by bud-grafting, from suckers or from marcotts. Spacing between trees should be 10 to 12 m (33 to 39 ft). Seedlings fruit for the first time at five to six years of age, but vegetatively-propagated trees may fruit two years after planting.

Rambutans usually fruit twice a year, and there are a number of named varieties in Malaysia and Indonesia.

General uses and recipes
Rambutan fruits have a high vitamin C content. They can be used fresh as a dessert, stewed, as a jam and in preserves.

RAMBUTAN DESSERT

ripe rambutans	water
sugar	sultanas
chopped nuts	

Wash the rambutans, nip off the stems, make an opening in the skin and squeeze out the flesh. Catch all the juice in a bowl. Place the flesh and the juice in a pan and add one tablespoon of water to one cup of rambutan juice. Add sugar to taste and simmer the mixture for 5 minutes. Cool. Add sultanas to the cooling fruit. Sprinkle the nuts over the cooled fruit before serving.

RAMBUTAN ICE-CREAM

ripe rambutans   vanilla ice-cream
whipped cream

Wash the rambutans, nip off the stems, make a slit in the skin and squeeze out the flesh. Chill the fruit, then pour it into individual glasses. Put a scoop of the ice-cream in each glass and top each with whipped cream.

RAMBUTAN JAM

450 g (1 lb) ripe rambutans   water
340 g (¾ lb) sugar   3 cloves

Wash the rambutans, nip off the stems, make a slit in the skin and squeeze out the flesh and the juice. Put the fruit and juice in a pan, add sufficient water to cover it and boil until the flesh separates from the seeds. Allow it to cool. Separate the seeds from the pulp and remove their thin skins. Add water to cover the seeds and boil them until soft. Drain. Add them to the pulp. Pour the sugar over the fruit and boil together for 20 minutes. Add the cloves to the hot jam. Test for setting. When the jam is cooked remove the cloves. Bottle in sterile jars.

25 *Rozelle* *Hibiscus sabdariffa*

Other names that may be used

Other English: Jamaica sorrel, red sorrel, sorrel, sour-sour
Indian subcontinent languages: pulincha-kira (Tamil); rata-bilincha (Singalese)
Portuguese: azedinha, vinagreira (Brazil)
Southeast Asian languages: krah jeub (Thai)
Spanish: flor de Jamaica (Mexico); viñuela (Panama)
West African languages: abema (Ewe); amukan (Yoruba); fol-lere (Fula); gurguza,
    sure, yakuwa (Hausa); ka-santhor (Temne); aja (Ibo); sakpa (Ga); sato
    (Mende); sawa-sawa, sorel (Creole)

Where it grows
Rozelle thrives in medium-rainfall areas of the tropics up to elevations of 1220 m
(4000 ft) and is most commonly cultivated in Sudan, West Africa and in the West
Indies.

Description
The rozelle is a robust, erect and branched annual herb, 1 to 2 m (3 to 6½ ft)

120

in height with purple stems. There is a green variety that grows taller, but this is used as a fibre plant. The leaves are 8 to 12 cm (3 to 5 in) in length, alternate and variable in shape according to their position on the stem. The flowers are single, dark red or light yellow and borne on short stalks on leafy axils. The fruit, oval and containing three or four dark-brown seeds, is enclosed in large, fleshy, succulent red sepals that remain and enlarge after the flower has fallen away. It is these that are used. They have a pleasing but very acid flavour.

Origin and history
The rozelle is probably indigenous to West Africa and was imported into the Americas at the time of the slave trade. It was first recorded in Brazil in the seventeenth century and in Jamaica in 1707. Although it has been imported into the Indian subcontinent and Southeast Asia, it has not spread very rapidly.

Notes on cultivation
This plant requires a deep, well-drained fertile soil if it is to thrive. It is usually grown from seed, though it can be propagated from cuttings. The seed can be broadcast, and the plants thinned out as is practised in West Africa, or seedlings may be planted at 1-1 1/5 m (3 to 4 ft) intervals.

Fruit is picked when the fleshy base of the flower is tender and plump, which should be about five to six months after planting or 15 to 20 days after flowering. Individual plants will yield up to 1½ kg (3 lb) of fruit.

General uses and recipes
The fruit contains approximately four per cent citric acid. It can be boiled with sugar to produce a drink or used to make jam, jellies or chutneys and preserves. The tender leaves and stalks can be eaten as a salad or added for seasoning to curries. In the Philippines it is used in *sinigang*, a fish or meat dish that includes acid-tasting leaves.

ROZELLE JAM

2¾ kg (6 lb) unripe rozelles   water
preserving sugar

Wash the fruits, cut them open and remove the centres with the seeds. Weigh. For each 1½ kg (3 lb) of the prepared rozelles, allow 2 cups of water. Place the prepared fruit in a preserving pan. Pour the water over the fruit and cook for 1 hour, until the pulp is soft. Cool. Measure the volume of the pulp. For each cup of pulp use 1¼ cups of sugar. Cook the pulp and the sugar together for 20 minutes. Test it for setting, and when it is ready store it in sterile jars.

ROZELLE JELLY

unripe rozelles   water
white sugar

Wash the rozelles and place them in a basin. Pour water over the fruit and leave
it to stand overnight. Slightly squeeze the fruit the next morning and pour the
mixture into a preserving pan. Boil until the fruit becomes pulpy. Strain the pulp
through a muslin bag, allowing the juice to drip slowly into a container. Measure
the volume of juice. To each 570 ml (1 pint) of the juice allow 450 g (1 lb)
of white sugar. Mix the juice and sugar in a preserving pan and simmer together
for 15 to 20 minutes until the jelly sets. Store in sterile jars.

26 Santol *Sandoricum koetjape*

Other names that may be used

Other botanical names: Sandoricum indicum, Sandoricum nervosum
Other English: yellow sentul, sweet sentul
Southeast Asian languages: kechapi, ketapi, sentul, sentiek (Malaysian); ka-thon
   (Thai); santol, santor, katul (Philippine languages)

Where it grows
Santol trees grow in the humid tropics up to an elevation of 914 m (3000 ft),
mainly in Southeast Asia and particularly in Indonesia, Malaysia and the
Philippines.

Description
The santol is a large, handsome tree with a smooth, straight trunk that grows as
high as 25 m (82 ft). The leaves are large, medium-green and divided into three
leaflets. They turn yellow or red, once a year, before they fall.
   The flowers are small and greenish-yellow, and hang in loose clusters. The

yellow fruits also hang this way and from a distance resemble oranges. They are slightly flattened at one end, and the skin, which is usually thick, has longitudinal wrinkles and exudes a thin milky juice when damaged. A translucent or pale, sweetish-acid pulp surrounds the large seeds. In Malaysia and the Philippines there are two types of santol. One has a thinner rind and is considered sweeter.

Origin and history
This fruit appears to have originated in the Malay archipelago and is seldom found outside Southeast Asia.

Notes on cultivation
Santol trees are cultivated, but they also grow wild in Malaysia, the Philippines and Indonesia. There is minimal knowledge as to the most suitable methods of cultivation.

SANTOLADE

10 ripe santols
4 cups water

1 cup white sugar

Wash, peel and seed the santols. Cut the fruit into small pieces. Mix the sugar into the fruit and mash the mixture with a fork. Pour the water over the fruit and stir vigorously. Allow to stand for 30 minutes. Stir again and serve chilled.

SANTOL JUICE

680 g (1½ lb) santol seed (from the *Candied Santol* recipe)

1.1 l (2 pints) water
115 g (4 oz) white sugar

Place the water in a preserving pan. Add the santol seeds and boil for 15 minutes. Strain through a muslin bag. Add the sugar to the juice and boil until it dissolves. Put the juice into jars and heat these half-sealed in a boiling water-bath. Seal the jars completely and store. This will keep for 1-3 months if refrigerated.

SANTOLS IN SYRUP

20 large ripe santols
1 kg (2 lb) preserving sugar

fresh water

sufficient 'rice-washing water' to cover the fruit twice. (Use water in which rice has been washed for the second or third time or water in which potatoes have been boiled.)

Wash the santols, place them in a preserving pan and cover with fresh water. Boil until tender, avoid breaking the skins. Drain the fruit and allow it to cool. Peel the santols, cut them into halves and remove the seeds. Cover the fruit with the rice-washing water and soak it overnight. This process prevents discolouration and removes the astringency. The treatment should be repeated after the fruit has been rinsed in fresh water. Soak overnight once again. Now cover the fruit with sufficient fresh water to let the santols float freely. Bring the water to the boil and drop the fruit into it. Boil for 5 minutes. Drain off the water. Dissolve the sugar in 570 ml (1 pint) fresh water and boil the syrup until it forms a thread when dropped from a spoon into a cup of cold water. Add the santols to the syrup. Boil for 10 minutes, then allow them to stand overnight. Drain the syrup into a preserving pan and bring it to the boil. Add the fruit and boil for 3 minutes. Store in sterile jars.

CANDIED SANTOL

25 ripe santols   water
preserving sugar

Wash the fruit, cover it with boiling water and leave it for 7 minutes. Rinse in cold water. Peel the fruits, cut them into halves and remove the seeds. Retain the seeds for use in the Santol Juice on page 124. Add 680 g (1½ lb) of sugar to 1.1 l (2 pints) of water in a preserving pan, then add the fruit and bring the mixture to the boil. Cool. Allow it to stand in a bowl overnight. Drain the syrup from the fruit into the pan. Add a further 340 g (12 oz) of sugar to the syrup and bring to the boil. Add the fruit and boil again. Cool. Store the mixture overnight in a basin. Three times more, reinforce the syrup with 340 g (12 oz) of sugar, and repeat the boiling, cooling and resting stages. Drain the fruit until no syrup drips from it. Wrap each piece of fruit in wax paper or cellophane. Store in air-tight jars.

SANTOL CHUTNEY

12 santols
1 clove garlic
1 cup chopped onion
⅓ cup scraped and chopped fresh
   ginger root
1½ cups preserving sugar

1 cup water
1 cup each red peppers and green
   peppers
1 cup raisins
3 cups vinegar
30 g (1 oz) salt

Place the santols in a preserving pan, pour the water over the fruit and boil for 10 minutes. Drain and cool. Peel the fruit, cut it into quarters and remove the seeds. Peel and crush the garlic, seed and slice the peppers into strips and add both, with the onion, to the santols. Mix the ginger root and the raisins with the fruit and pack the mixture into jars. Mix together the vinegar, sugar and salt in a pan and bring to the boil. Pour the boiling liquid over the fruit mixture and seal while hot. Serve after 3 days.

27 Soursop *Anona muricata*

Other names that may be used

Dutch: zuurzak
French: cachiman-épineux, corossel, corosellier, corossol épineux, sappadille
Indian subcontinent languages: katu-anoda (Singalese); seetha (Tamil)
Pacific languages: seremaia (Fijian)
Portuguese: araticu-ponhé; coraçao de Rainha; groviola; jaca do Pará (Brazil)
Southeast Asian languages: durian belanda, durian europa, durian maki
   (Malaysian); guayabano (Tagalog); sirsat (Indonesian); tha-rian-khaek (Thai)
Spanish: guanábana
West African languages: aduantunkum (Twi); alukutum (Krobo); vo, votsi (Ewe)

Where it grows
Soursop trees are widely grown in the humid tropics up to an altitude of 1000 m
(3300 ft), but probably thrive best in oceanic tropical islands.

Description

The soursop is a quick-growing evergreen tree, approximately 7½ m (25 ft) in height when mature, with a short, brown-barked trunk that is often warty. Branches emerge near the base of the tree and as it ages the tree becomes very straggly. The leathery leaves are 6 to 18 cm (2 to 7 in) long and 2½ to 7 cm (1 to 3 in) wide with a dark, glossy, green surface and a dull and pale underside. The quite large, strongly-scented flowers are greenish to pale yellow and are borne on short, two-flower twigs.

Fruits, that may weigh as much as 3 ⅔ kg (8 lb), are borne on thick, woody stalks. They are often kidney-shaped, but there are many curious variations as the fruit is sometimes constricted in shape, owing to some of the ovules being unfertilized. The thick skin is dark green and has rows of soft, green spines. The fruit is soft when ripe, has a strong but pleasant scent and bruises easily. The pulpy flesh is creamy white and juicy, has a very characteristic sweet-sour taste and contains some soft fibres and many black shiny seeds.

Origin and history

Like other members of the *Anona* genus, the soursop was originally indigenous to tropical America.

Notes on cultivation

The tree appears to grow quite well on a variety of soils. It is usually propagated from seed but may also be budded. The planting distance is 6^2 m (20^2 ft). Age at first fruiting is three to four years, and the trees require little pruning. In the lowland tropics flowering and fruiting continue throughout the year.

General uses and recipes

Soursops are a particularly rich source of vitamin C. They are used in the same manner as custard apples, but because of their sweet-sour flavour the ice-cream made from them has a very special, delicious flavour.

SOURSOP COCKTAIL

1 medium ripe soursop	1 lemon
1 wine-glass gin	a dash of brandy
sugar	

Peel the fruit and squeeze it through a fine sieve. Retain the liquor. Extract the juice from the lemon and add to the soursop liquor. Add the gin, brandy and sugar to taste to the mixture. Mix, chill and serve.

SOURSOP ICED DRINK

1 medium, ripe soursop
1 cup white sugar
a few drops of green food colouring

3½ l (6 pints) water
½ cup lemon or kalamansi juice

Peel the soursop. Add 1.1 l (2 pints) of the water to the fruit and squeeze the fruit in the water. Strain, retaining the liquor. Add the remaining water, with the sugar and the lemon juice to the fruit liquor and mix well. Stir in the colouring, mix again and serve the drink well iced.

SOURSOP ICE-CREAM

soursops
½ tablespoon gelatine crystals or
   powder
1 cup chilled evaporated milk

2 tablespoons cold water
½ cup boiling water
1 cup white sugar

Peel the fruit and press it through a fine sieve; measure 1 cup of the liquor. Add the cold water to the gelatine in a basin. Add the boiling water and stir until the gelatine dissolves. Pour the soursop liquor into the gelatine solution. Stir. Add the sugar and stir until it dissolves. Whip the milk and fold it into the mixture. Pour into ice-trays and put in the freezer for 2 hours.

SOURSOP CHARLOTTE

1 large, firm, ripe soursop
½ cup sugar
grated nutmeg to taste

2 cups dried breadcrumbs
3 tablespoons butter or margarine

Peel, core and chop the fruit, removing the seeds. Place one-third of the fruit in a greased pie dish. Cover the fruit with one-third of the breadcrumbs. Sprinkle one-third of the sugar over the breadcrumbs. Dot one-third of the butter over the breadcrumbs. Sprinkle nutmeg over the breadcrumbs. Repeat this twice, until all the fruit is used. Bake in an oven at 180°C (350°F), Gas Mark 4 until it is golden brown (approximately 20 minutes). Serve with cream or custard.

SOURSOP FOOL

1 medium, ripe soursop
20 marshmallows
1 cup thick cream *or* 1 cup chilled and whipped evaporated milk

¼ cup water
2 tablespoons white sugar

Peel the fruit and squeeze it through a sieve. Measure out 1 cup of the liquor. Pour the water into a basin immersed in a saucepan of hot water. Add the marshmallows and stir until they have dissolved. Add the sugar and again stir until it has dissolved. Mix the soursop liquor with the marshmallow mixture and cool until the mixture is partly set. Fold the cream into the mixture. Serve chilled.

SOURSOP SHERBET

1 egg white	1 medium, ripe soursop
2 cups water	1 cup white sugar
1 tablespoon lemon juice	

Lightly whip the egg white and half-freeze. Peel the fruit and squeeze it through a sieve. Measure out 2 cups of the liquor. Place the water in a saucepan. Add the sugar, boil for 5 minutes and cool until the syrup is lukewarm. Fold in the soursop liquor, lemon juice and egg white. Freeze in a serving dish.

SOURSOP JELLY

1 medium, ripe soursop	1.1 l (2 pints) water
white sugar	lemon juice

Peel the soursop and place it in a saucepan. Pour the water over the fruit and boil for 15 minutes. Strain through a muslin bag and measure the volume of the liquor. For each 570 ml (1 pint) of fruit liquor allow 340 g (12 oz) of sugar and 2 tablespoons of lemon juice. Boil the sugar and liquor together briskly for 10 minutes. Add the lemon juice and reboil briskly for 10 more minutes or until the jelly sets. Store in sterile jars.

28 Star Apple *Chrysophyllum cainito*

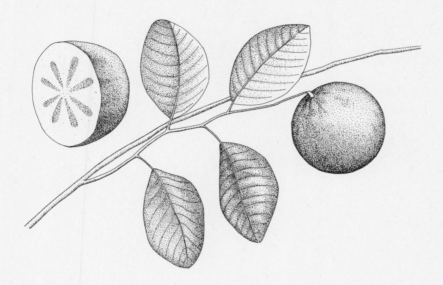

Other names that may be used

Other English: sugar apple
Indian subcontinent languages: rata-lawulu (Singalese); seemaipala-pallam (Tamil)
Southeast Asian languages: caimito (Tagalog)
Spanish: caimito

Where it grows
The star apple is cultivated mainly in tropical Latin America, the West Indies and Southeast Asia, but as it is considered to be an ornamental, isolated trees are found everywhere in the lowland tropics.

Description
The star-apple is a medium-sized, strikingly ornamental tree with a spreading crown and beautiful leaves that are a shiny dark-green on the top surface and copper-coloured underneath.

The flowers are small and purplish-brown, and the fruit, which may vary in shape but is usually round and approximately the size of a large orange, can be green or a deep-purple when ripe. The skin contains an unpleasant-tasting latex

131

and encloses a white, sweet edible pulp in which a number of small, hard, brown glossy seeds are embedded. If the fruit is cut at right-angles to the stalk, the central core resembles a star — hence its name.

Origin and history
It is presumed that it originated from the West Indies or Central America.

Notes on cultivation
This tree is normally propagated from seed, and if it is planted in an orchard, the spacing should be 12 m (40 ft) either way. It fruits at four to six years of age and mature trees will produce as many as 300 fruits.

General uses and recipes
It is normally used in desserts.

STAR APPLE DESSERT

4 star apples
140 ml (¼ pint) double cream *or*
    sweetened condensed milk

3 oranges
white sugar
a dash of rum (optional)

Cut the star apples into halves and remove the pips. Scoop out the pulp and put it into a blender. Peel the oranges and remove the pips and pith. Add the flesh to the star apples and blend together. Whip the cream or condensed milk and add to the fruit, together with sugar to taste. Stir the rum into the mixture and chill. Serve in individual glasses.

29 Tamarind *Tamarindus indica*

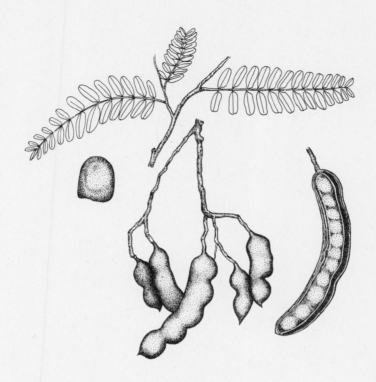

Other names that may be used

Indian subcontinent languages: siyambala (Singalese)
Southeast Asian languages: asam (Indonesian); ma kharm (Thai); asam jawa
    (Malaysian); sampalok (Tagalog)
Spanish: chita, tamarindo

Where it grows
Tamarind is particularly well adapted to the semi-arid tropical regions, but it also thrives in the monsoon tropics on well-drained soils. It is common in semi-arid tropical Africa and Western Asia and in monsoon Asia, and is found almost everywhere in drier regions of the tropics.

Description
The tamarind is a large handsome semi-evergreen tree that on average grows as tall as 20 m (66 ft). It has a compact symmetrical crown with drooping branches, and the trunk, often twisted, has grey scaly bark. The leaves are 7 to 15 cm (3 to

6 in) long, lacy and divided into small leaflets. The flowers are very small, yellow-ish with pink strips and occur in drooping bunches, 5 to 10 cm (2 to 4 in) long, at the end of twigs.

As the tree is a legume, it produces pods. These are 5 to 10 cm (2 to 4 in) long, scurfy brown in colour, with a brittle shell. The pods contain one to ten seeds that are joined to each other by tough fibres in a mass of sweetish, acid, brown pulp. It is this pulp that is used in cooking.

Origin and history
Tamarind trees grow wild in the semi-arid, tropical savannas of Africa. They must have been introduced into Western Asia and India at an early date. Today the tamarind trees of India are improved varieties of the wild African tree.

Notes on cultivation
Tamarinds appear to thrive on very poor soils in the tropical African savanna, but it is noticeable that they often grow adjacent to a termite mound.

The tree is normally propagated from seed but it can be budded or propagated from cuttings. When the tree is cultivated, the planting distance is 12 m (40 ft). Seedlings first fruit at seven to eight years of age.

General uses and recipes
The brown pulp from ripe tamarinds contains approximately ten per cent tartaric acid, giving it a decidedly acid flavour. It also contains a high percentage of carbohydrates that are present mainly in the form of sugars, though approximately three per cent of the pulp is fibre. The pulp is sold pressed and preserved, when it looks like squashed dates.

Pressed pulp can be used to make a refreshing drink or sherbet, jams etc. It can be eaten with meat as a condiment or used as an ingredient of chutney and of preserves. Mixed with sugar it makes a sweetmeat. It is generally agreed that the pulp acts as a gentle laxative.

The leaves and flowers can be used in salads, soups and curries. The seeds can be eaten roasted or boiled and are sometimes boiled, dried and pounded to make a flour. Twigs are used as toothbrushes in many parts of southern and southeastern Asia.

Wood from the tamarind makes excellent charcoal and the hard red timber is prized as a cabinet wood. Tamarind is both an ornamental and excellent shade tree.

CANDIED TAMARIND

plump, ripe tamarinds	white sugar
water	

Do not wash the tamarinds. Remove the shell, retaining the stem to keep the fruit's shape. Place the fruit in a bowl. Dissolve 1 cup of the sugar in 1 cup of water by boiling for 1 to 2 minutes. Cool the syrup and pour it over the fruit. Cover the bowl with greaseproof paper and weigh it down with an inverted plate. Leave to soak for 3 to 4 days. Make a thicker syrup by boiling 2 cups of white sugar in 1 cup of water. Pour it over the drained fruit and cover as before, leaving the mixture to stand for 2 to 3 days. Taste the fruit, and if it is not sufficiently sweet drain off the syrup and measure the volume. For each cup of syrup, add 1 cup of sugar. Boil the combined syrup and sugar mixture quickly and cool. Pour the mixture over the fruit and cover again, leaving it for 1 to 2 days. Drain the syrup. Place the fruit on a wire rack and dry it in the sun for 2 days. (Alternatively place the fruit in an oven kept at the lowest setting for 30 minutes.) Repeat one day later. When the drying is completed, the fruit should be slightly sticky and chewy. Wrap each piece of fruit in waxed paper or cellophane and store in air-tight jars.

TAMARIND PASTE

ripe, fleshy tamarinds
sweet potatoes
castor sugar

water
sugar

Shell the tamarinds and break the flesh into pieces. Place it in a saucepan and cover with water. Boil and stir until the flesh separates from the seeds. Strain the fruit and press it through a coarse sieve. Discard the residue. Measure the volume of pulp. Wash, peel, boil and mash the sweet potatoes. Measure the volume: for each ½ cup of tamarind pulp use an equal quantity of potato and 1 cup of sugar. Cook the tamarind pulp and potato together, stirring constantly, until the mixture becomes as thick as jam. Add the sugar and continue boiling and stirring until the mixture leaves the side of the pan. Test by dropping a teaspoonful of paste into a cup of cold water. If the paste keeps its shape it will be ready. Cool the mixture by standing the pan in a bowl of cold water. Scoop out teaspoonfuls of the paste and roll them into balls with greased hands. Drop them on to a plate of castor sugar and roll them around to cover them with sugar. Wrap each ball in waxed paper or cellophane and store in air-tight jars.

TAMARIND AND PAPAYA JAM

ripe tamarinds
ripe papayas

water
preserving sugar

Shell the tamarinds, break the flesh into pieces, cover with water and leave to soak overnight. Boil the fruit in the water until the flesh separates from the seeds. Press through a coarse sieve and retain the pulp. Measure the volume. Peel the papayas and remove the seeds. Press the flesh through a coarse sieve and retain the pulp. Measure the volume. For each cup of tamarind pulp allow an equal amount of papaya pulp and 3 cups of sugar. Mix or blend the pulps together and place in a pan. Pour the sugar over the pulps and boil all together for 10 mintues. When it has reached setting point, seal it in sterile jars.

TAMARINDO

ripe tamarinds   water
sugar

Shell the tamarinds, break the flesh into pieces, cover them with water and let them soak overnight. Then boil them in the water until the flesh separates from the seeds. Press it through a coarse sieve and measure it. For each cup of pulp, allow an equal amount of sugar. Mix the sugar with the pulp in a pan and boil until the mixture thickens. Store in sterile jars. Serve with curry, ice-cream or desserts.

TAMARIND SYRUP

ripe tamarinds   water
white sugar

Shell the tamarinds and break the flesh into pieces. Measure the volume. For 2 cups of the tamarind flesh, allow 6 cups of water and 5½ cups of sugar. Pour the water over the tamarinds in a bowl and leave them to soak overnight. Place the sugar in a preserving pan and add the soaked tamarinds. Boil for 15 minutes. Strain them and rub the flesh through a sieve. Heat the resulting syrup to boiling point and store it in sterile jars. To serve, dilute a cup of syrup with 4 cups of water and add a sprig of mint and ice; alternatively add 1 teaspoon of syrup to a glass of iced fizzy lemonade.

TAMARIND BALLS

ripe tamarinds   sugar
tamarind seeds   castor sugar

Shell the tamarinds and scrape the pulp off the seeds. Weigh the pulp. Retain the seeds. For each 115 g (4 oz) of tamarind pulp, allow 450 g (1 lb) of sugar. Mix the tamarind pulp with the sugar, kneading it well until the mixture is light in colour. Cover each seed with sufficient of the mixture to make a ball. Roll the balls in castor sugar. Store in air-tight containers.

30 Tree Tomato *Cyphomandra betacea*

Other names that may be used

Other botanical names: Solanum betaceum, Solanum fragrans
Dutch: struiktomaat
French: tomate d'arbe
Indian subcontinent languages: gas-takkali (Singalese)
Portuguese: tomate francês
Southeast Asian languages: terong belanda (Indonesian)
Spanish: tomate arbol

Where it grows
This small tree is found throughout the tropical highlands of the world where it
thrives at altitudes from 1000 m (3300 ft) upwards. It is particularly common in
the Andean countries of South America, East Africa and Southeast Asia. It also
grows quite well in subtropical lowlands and in warm temperate regions, such as
the northern island of New Zealand.

138

Description

The tree tomato is a semi-woody evergreen shrub or small, 1¾ to 3 m (6 to 10 ft), tree with grey bark and large, broad, pointed leaves borne near the end of the branches.

The flowers are small, fragrant and pink or light blue. The fruit, which is egg shaped and smooth skinned, is produced in great abundance in clusters at the end of the young shoots. All fruits are greenish-purple before ripening, but one type ripens to a deep purple and the other to a reddish-yellow. The flesh is slightly acid and succulent, contains many seeds, may be pink or yellow and is somewhat similar in flavour to the tomato.

Origin and history

A native of the Andean region of Peru, the tree tomato has been introduced to other upland regions of the tropics and to subtropical lowland areas since the conquest of Peru by the Spaniards.

Notes on cultivation

The tree tomato requires a deep, fertile, moist soil. It can be grown from seed or cuttings and is sometimes propagated by budding. If planted in an orchard, the spacing should be 2 to 3 m (6½ to 10 ft). It is a vigorous, quick-growing tree that fruits at 1½ to 2 years of age and continues to bear for five to six years. In the high altitude tropics, it fruits throughout the year, yielding some 20 kg (44 lb) of fruit per tree.

General uses and recipes

Some people enjoy eating the fresh fruit, but it is usually stewed or used for jelly or chutney.

STEWED TREE TOMATOES

ripe tree tomatoes	water
white sugar	

Wash the tree tomatoes and place them in a pan. Cover the fruit with water and bring to the boil. Add sugar to taste and simmer until the fruit is soft. Serve as you would stewed plums.

TREE TOMATO JELLY

ripe tree tomatoes water
preserving sugar

Wash and quarter the tree tomatoes. Cover the fruit with water and boil until
the fruit becomes mushy. Strain and remove all seeds and skin. Weigh the pulp
and return it to the pan. For each 450 g (1 lb) of pulp, allow 340 g (12 oz) of
sugar. Add the sugar to the pulp and boil until the mixture thickens. Test for
setting, and when setting point is achieved, pour the jelly into sterile jars.

TREE TOMATO CHUTNEY

1¾ kg (4 lb) tree tomatoes 1.1 l (2 pints) vinegar
1½ kg (3 lb) preserving sugar 1 kg (2 lb) raisins
115 g (4 oz) garlic of shallots a pinch of salt
cayenne pepper

Wash and slice the tree tomatoes. Place the vinegar and the tomatoes in a
preserving pan and bring to the boil. Dissolve the sugar in the fruit mixture and
simmer until it becomes jam-like. Put the raisins through a mincer and add
them to the fruit. Peel and chop the garlic or shallots finely and add them to the
mixture. Season with salt and a small amount of cayenne. Boil the chutney for
5 minutes. Bottle hot into sterile jars and seal.

Index